SUN VALLEY COOKBOOK

Moritz Community Hospital Auxiliary

SUN VALLEY COOKBOOK

Moritz Community Hospital Auxiliary

FOREWORD BY
W. AVERELL HARRIMAN

INTRODUCTION BY
DORICE TAYLOR

PEANUT BUTTER
PUBLISHING

Seattle, Washington

The proceeds from the sale of this book will be returned to **Moritz Community Hospital** through the Moritz Community Hospital Auxiliary.

For additional copies, please use the order blanks in the back of the book or write directly to:

> **Moritz Community Hospital Auxiliary**
> **P.O. Box 555**
> **Sun Valley, Idaho 83353**

Checks should be made payable to **Moritz Community Hospital Auxiliary** for the amount of $9.95 plus $2.00 postage and handling per copy. Idaho residents please add 40 cents (4%) tax per copy.

Sun Valley Cookbook may be obtained for fundraising projects or by retail outlets at special rates. Write above address for further information.

Cover watercolor by Don Bemco Bennett
Chapter photographs by Steve Snyder
Design by Advertising Associates of Sun Valley
Edited by Marcia Green and the Hospital Auxiliary
Production by April Ryan

ISBN 0-89716-138-6

ACKNOWLEDGMENTS

Moritz Community Hospital Auxiliary Board

Editors
Michelle Praggastis   Suzanne Manookian   Roxanne Sanderson

Proofreaders
Connie Grabow   Pat Ennis   Ritu Shivdasani   Christina Potters

Ann Boughton	Pat Gwinner
Sue Bridgman	Carol Jones
Janet Brown	Donna Kelsey
D.J. Cahen	Diane Kneeland
Jane Chesley	Jo Ann Levy
Cathy Crosson	Lorie Luber
Valerie Dumke	Winki McCray
Janet Dunbar	Fran Monahan
Barbara Dutcher	Cicely Nicolai
Judy Ferries	Betsy Ohrstrom
Sheila Fryberger	Gertrude Potters
Louise Gallagher	Jean Ray
Nietz Gray	Gayle Stevenson

The Moritz Community Hospital Auxiliary Board would like to thank
all the members and friends of the hospital who shared their favorite recipes
and spent endless hours in the kitchen testing them.

The Board is especially grateful to Edmund W. Dumke
for his encouragement and for underwriting the printing
of our first edition.

W. AVERELL HARRIMAN

From the beginning of Sun Valley in 1936, I thought it essential to take care of those who got hurt skiing or became ill while here. I take great satisfaction knowing that Sun Valley has always had fine medical care available to everyone, and I am so pleased that the hospital has maintained the highest standards. It is vital to the well-being of our community that we provide the finest facilities and personnel we can. I commend all of you who are contributing to this effort to make the Sun Valley hospital an exceptionally good institution.

I think Sun Valley is one of the great resorts in America, and I also think many of these recipes are great too!

My thanks to all of you who are working—and cooking—and eating well—for helping to make the Sun Valley hospital the excellent one it is.

W. AVERELL HARRIMAN

CONTENTS

SUN VALLEY LODGE
OPENING DINNER
DECEMBER 21, 1936

BRIOCHE AU CAVIAR

BEEF TEA DES VIVEURS
PAILLETTES DOREES

SUPREME OF SOLE AU CHAMPAGNE VALLEY LODGE

TOURNEDOS—SAUTE—CHATELAINE
POMME MASCOTTE
HARICOTS VERTS FINS AU GRATIN

SALADE DES ILES

ANANAS SURPRISE, UNION PACIFIQUE
FRIVOLITES AMERICAINES

CAFE DES PRINCES

ACCOMPANIMENTS:
WITH BRIOCHE—MANHATTAN COCKTAIL
WITH ENTRÉE—MOSELLE
WITH DESSERT—CHAMPAGNE
AFTER DINNER—CIGARES AND LIQUEURS

SUN VALLEY INN
Chef's Suggestion — 60 Cents

Filet of Halibut Saute, Julienne Potatoes, Cauliflower au gratin
Compote of Fresh Fruit   Beverage
OR
Creamed Flaked Turkey and Toast, Mashed Potatoes
Young Peas   Compote of Fresh Fruit   Beverage

HISTORICAL TIDBITS

We salute the members of the Moritz Community Hospital Auxiliary who have put together this cookbook. It will carry on the tradition of good cooking and fun dining in this community.

On the opposite page behold the menu of the opening dinner served at the Sun Valley Lodge on December 21, 1936. Many great dinners have been given at the Lodge, with much more elaborate menus, but none under more challenging circumstances.

Ground had not been broken for the building of the Sun Valley Lodge until the middle of June, 1936. Every bit of material, down to the last nail, had to be transported into this then-remote valley. But, in the amazing time of seven months the Lodge was built, furnished with custom-made furniture, staffed and ready for the opening on the 21st of December. There were a few problems to be solved before the Brioche au Caviar could be served. For instance, when the chief engineer on opening day went up to throw open the doors of the dining room, the handsome oak and copper doors would not budge. They had been hung upside down.

There is another menu worth noting. That is, if you consider that Sun Valley really dates from that stormy evening, January 16, 1936, when Count Felix Schaffgotsch arrived in Ketchum, then a wide spot in a road that went nowhere.

The Count, as you probably know, had been on a journey that took him from Mt. Rainier to Mt. Hood, to Tahoe, then to Colorado, Utah, Jackson Hole and eastern Idaho, looking for the perfect spot where Averell Harriman, chairman of the board of the Union Pacific Railroad, could build a ski resort that would equal the famous old resorts of Europe.

The watchman at the Bald Mountain Motel shoveled out a cabin for the party and the Golden Rule grocery opened its doors to provide what, according to his Union Pacific escort, were the Count's favorite ingredients for a meal. Sun Valley's first recorded dinner—coffee, bread, eggs and canned peaches.

In 1937 the Sun Valley Inn opened. This was Harriman's thoughtful answer to the problems of the young skiers who could not afford the Lodge. You will be interested in the price of the chef's suggestion for luncheon at the Continental Cafe.

Dorice Taylor

Director of Publicity for Sun Valley
1955 to 1971

APPETIZERS

APPETIZER CHEESE CAKE

Betsy Ohrstrom

Serves 12

2 tablespoons melted butter
1 (6 ounce) box cheese crackers, crushed
½ cup diced stuffed olives
½ cup diced celery
1 medium green pepper, diced
1 small onion, diced
2 tablespoons lemon juice
1 teaspoon salt
1 teaspoon Worcestershire sauce
¼ teaspoon paprika
Dash of liquid hot pepper
2 cups thick sour cream
Ripe olives cut into rings
Pimento strips

Brush sides and bottom of 9-inch springform pan with melted butter and press half the crushed cracker crumbs on bottom to form base. Combine stuffed olives, celery, green pepper, onion, lemon juice, salt, Worcestershire sauce, paprika, liquid hot pepper and sour cream. Blend well. Spread this mixture over cracker base. Scatter remaining crumbs over top. Cover and refrigerate for at least 24 hours. Remove pan side and place cake, still on pan bottom, on serving platter. Garnish top with ripe olives and pimento. Cut into wedges.

NIETZ'S CHEESE STICKS

Nietz Gray

Serves 6-8

1 cup flour
½ cup chilled butter
1 teaspoon mayonnaise
1 cup shredded cheddar cheese
1 tablespoon water
¼ teaspoon salt
1 teaspoon onion salt
1 teaspoon celery salt
1 teaspoon dried dill
½ cup sesame seeds (optional)

Place flour in a large mixing bowl, cut in butter until mixture resembles coarse meal. Add mayonnaise, cheese, water, salts, dill and sesame seeds (if desired). Mix well. Cover and chill at leat 2 hours.

On floured pastry board, roll out dough to ¼-inch thickness. Cut into finger-sized pieces. Twist each stick and place on non-stick or greased cookie sheet. Bake at 350° for 20-25 minutes or until lightly browned.

LADY ANNE'S CHEESE GLOBES

Penny Sherry

Makes 3 dozen

1 pound Swiss cheese, shredded
2 tablespoons chopped parsley
⅜ teaspoon nutmeg
⅝ teaspoon paprika
1 egg white
¼ cup flour
2 tablespoons plus ¼ teaspoon milk
1 egg
1 cup unseasoned bread crumbs
Peanut oil

Combine cheese, parsley, nutmeg and paprika with a fork. Whisk egg white until fluffy and blend well with cheese mixture. Chill 3 hours. Mix together flour, milk and egg. Mold cheese mixture into 1½-inch balls. Dip balls in egg mixture, then roll in bread crumbs. Refrigerate globes for 10 hours or overnight. Heat oil to 350°. Fry globes 4-5 minutes. Drain promptly on paper towels and serve.

These globes can be refrigerated and reheated at 400° for 12 minutes, but they will not be as crisp.

Variation   *Add ham, crab or artichoke hearts to the cheese mixture.*

FONDUE NEUCHATELOISE

Mrs. Hadley Stuart

Serves 4

¼ pound imported Swiss cheese, shredded
¼ pound imported Emmenthaler cheese, shredded
1 tablespoon flour
1 clove garlic, minced
1 cup dry white wine
3 tablespoons Kirsch
Salt and freshly ground pepper
Nutmeg
1 loaf sourdough French bread, cubed

In a mixing bowl, dredge cheeses with flour. Set aside. Place garlic and wine in a fondue pot. Bring to boil. Keeping wine hot, gradually stir in cheese mixture. When mixture boils again, add Kirsch and salt, pepper and nutmeg to taste. Keep hot. Serve with fondue forks and the cubed French bread.

SURPRISE CHEESE BALLS

Janet Dunbar

Makes 40 balls

1 cup shredded cheddar cheese
1 cup flour
½ cup softened butter
1 teaspoon Worcestershire sauce
1-2 drops Tabasco sauce
40 cocktail onions, or 40 small stuffed
    green olives, or combination of both

Combine cheese, flour, butter, Worcestershire and Tabasco sauce in a mixing bowl. Knead mixture until well combined and pliable. Form into 1-inch balls and press an onion or olive into center. Reshape ball to enclose onion or olive. Place on greased cookie sheet. Bake at 400° for 15 minutes or until lightly browned. Serve hot.

Can be frozen ahead and baked before serving.

❦❦❦❦

TIROPETA

Stephanie Gregores

Makes 10 dozen

½ pound feta cheese
½ pound Roquefort cheese
½ pound grated Parmesan cheese
8 ounces cottage cheese
5 eggs, beaten
1 pound filo dough
1½ cups melted butter

Place cheeses and eggs in a large mixing bowl and beat until well blended. Lay out 1 sheet of filo at a time, cut into 3x12-inch strips. Brush each strip lightly with melted butter. Place a rounded teaspoon of cheese filling on end of strip. Fold over the corner to make a triangle. Continue folding strip from side to side making a triangle (folding like a flag). Place triangles on lightly greased baking sheet and brush top with butter. Proceed in this manner with remaining filling and filo. Bake at 350° for 15 minutes or until golden brown. Serve hot. Freezes well.

❦❦❦❦

STUFFED MUSHROOMS

Margie Grimes

Serves 18-24

36 medium mushrooms
8 ounces cream cheese
6 strips bacon, cooked and crumbled
½ teaspoon Worcestershire sauce
¼ teaspoon onion powder

Clean and stem mushrooms, reserving stems. Finely chop stems. In a mixing bowl, combine stems, cream cheese, bacon, Worcestershire sauce and onion powder. Mix well. Divide mixture evenly among caps. Bake at 350° for 10-15 minutes or until browned. Serve hot.

MUSHROOM HORS D'OEUVRES

Pat Ennis

Makes 40 rounds

1 loaf firm white bread, sliced
8 ounces cream cheese, room temperature
1-2 tablespoons chopped onion
¼ teaspoon seasoning salt
2 egg yolks
Dash of Worcestershire sauce
½ cup melted butter
2 small jars mushroom caps,
    drained and dried
Paprika

Cut bread slices into 1½-inch rounds (use cookie cutter). Arrange on baking sheet. Set aside. Preheat broiler. Combine cream cheese, onion, seasoning salt, egg yolks and Worcestershire sauce. Mix well. Set aside.

Toast one side of bread rounds lightly under broiler. Turn untoasted side up and brush with melted butter. Place 1 mushroom cap on each round and divide filling among caps. Sprinkle with paprika. Broil carefully until lightly brown. Serve.

Rounds may be frozen before final broiling. Thaw 20 minutes and brown lightly.

MUSHROOM NACHOS

Glenn Janss

Serves 6-8

24 large mushrooms
4-6 tablespoons butter, melted
2 ounces pepperoni or chorizo sausage
1-2 Jalapeno peppers, diced
1½ cups shredded Monterey Jack
    or sharp cheddar cheese
1 small red bell pepper, roasted,
    or 2 canned pimentos, cut into 24 pieces
¼ cup minced green onion
Sour cream (optional)

Clean mushrooms with a damp paper towel. Remove stems and reserve for future use. Line baking sheet with foil. Brush mushroom caps on both sides with melted butter and arrange on baking sheet.

Preheat broiler. Cut sausage in half lengthwise and slice thinly into 24 pieces. Set 1 piece of sausage in each mushroom cap. Sprinkle with Jalapenos and shredded cheese. Top each cap with red pepper or pimento. Broil until cheese is melted. Sprinkle with green onion and serve with sour cream if desired.

As a first course for a Mexican party, mushrooms can be served in a nest of Fritos or nacho chips. A heated platter will help keep these warm.

COLD BASIL SHRIMP

Ruth Lieder
Mayor of Sun Valley

Serves 6

¾ cup olive oil
2 tablespoons lemon juice
1 tablespoon wine vinegar
1 tablespoon minced parsley
2 cloves garlic, crushed
2 tablespoons Dijon mustard
½ cup fresh basil leaves
½ teaspoon oregano
1 teaspoon salt
Freshly ground pepper to taste
2 pounds large shrimp in shells

Combine all ingredients, except shrimp, in a shallow pan. Mix well. Set aside. With kitchen scissors, split along back of each shrimp and devein. Place shrimp in marinade for at least 2 hours, turning frequently.

Thread shrimp on flat metal skewers and grill or broil for 3 minutes on each side or until just cooked. Cool. Serve shrimp in their shells with plenty of napkins.

Absolutely fantastic! A Pettit Lake specialty!!

COCKTAIL PARTY SHRIMP

Jeanne Burggraf

Serves 15-20

3 pounds large shrimp, shelled, deveined
⅔-1 cup mayonnaise
2 tablespoons heavy cream
2 tablespoons tarragon vinegar
2 tablespoons dried parsley flakes
2 tablespoons minced onion
½ teaspoon celery seed
½ teaspoon sweet basil
½ teaspoon salt
¼ teaspoon pepper

Put shrimp in saucepan large enough to hold shrimp comfortably and cover with water. Bring to boil and cook until shrimp become opaque and turn pink. Do not overcook. Drain. Set aside to cool. When cool, pat dry.

Combine remaining ingredients in mixing bowl. Add cooled shrimp. Cover tightly and marinate overnight, stirring occasionally. Serve in a chilled bowl. Do not drain.

I use a sealed Tupperware bowl to marinate shrimp and invert occasionally.

ROQUEFORT STUFFED SHRIMP

Cassie Majerus

Serves 8-10

2 quarts salted water
24 jumbo shrimp
3 ounces cream cheese
1 ounce Roquefort or Danish blue cheese
½ teaspoon prepared mustard
1 teaspoon minced scallions or chives
1 cup fresh minced parsley
½ teaspoon dried dill
    or 1 teaspoon fresh dill

Bring salted water to rolling boil and add shrimp. Cook 3-4 minutes or until opaque. Rinse immediately under cold water. Drain, peel and split shrimp down top side about half way through. Chill. Blend cream cheese, Roquefort, mustard and scallions. Using a knife and small spatula, stuff cheese mixture into the split backs of the shrimp. Mix together parsley and dill. Roll the cheese side of the shrimp in the parsley and dill. Serve chilled.

A delectable appetizer.

❦

SHRIMP RING

Connie Beck

Serves 12

1 envelope unflavored gelatin
3-4 tablespoons water
1 can tomato soup, undiluted
8 ounces cream cheese
½ cup chopped onion
½ cup chopped celery
½ cup chopped green pepper
1 cup mayonnaise
2 (6 ounce) cans shrimp, or more if desired

Soften gelatin in water. Heat soup to boiling. Add softened gelatin and stir until dissolved. Remove from heat. Add cream cheese and combine well. Cool slightly. Add onion, celery, green pepper, mayonnaise and shrimp. Pour into lightly greased 6-cup mold and chill until firm. Dip in hot water to unmold. Serve with crackers.

❦

CHINESE BAR-B-QUED CHICKEN WINGS

Nancy Humphrey

Serves 6

12 chicken wings
Hoisin sauce
Garlic powder
Coarsely ground black pepper

Place chicken wings on grill. Paint with Hoisin sauce and sprinkle with garlic powder and pepper. When cooked on one side, turn, paint with sauce and sprinkle with garlic powder and pepper. Cook until done.

SPINACH-WRAPPED CHICKEN WITH ORIENTAL DIP

Judy Smooke

Serves 6-8

1¾ cups chicken broth
¼ cup soy sauce
1 tablespoon Worcestershire sauce
2 whole chicken breasts
1 pound fresh spinach
Lettuce leaves

ORIENTAL DIP
1 cup sour cream
2 teaspoons sesame seeds, toasted
½ teaspoon ground ginger
4 teaspoons soy sauce
2 teaspoons Worcestershire sauce

In a 3 quart saucepan, bring broth, soy sauce and Worcestershire sauce to boil. Add chicken and simmer until tender, about 20 minutes. Remove from heat, drain chicken, set aside to cool. Remove skin and bones. Cut into 1-inch cubes.

Wash spinach thoroughly and remove stems. Place leaves in colander and pour 3-4 quarts boiling water over them. Drain thoroughly and cool. To assemble, place a chicken piece at stem end of leaf, veined side up. Roll over once. Fold leaf in on both sides and continue rolling. Secure each end with a toothpick. Chill. Cover serving plate with lettuce leaves. Place ORIENTAL DIP in a small bowl in the center. Surround with spinach wrapped chicken.

ORIENTAL DIP   Combine all ingredients in a small bowl. Chill at least 4 hours to blend flavors.

MANHATTAN MEATBALLS

**Sheila Fryberger
Dates Fryberger**
  1964 U.S. Olympic Hockey Team

Serves 8-10

1 pound ground pork
1 pound ground beef
½ cup chopped onions
2 tablespoons chopped parsley
2 teaspoons salt
2 eggs, slightly beaten

SAUCE
10 ounce jar apricot preserves
½ cup barbecue sauce

In a mixing bowl combine pork, beef, onions, parsley, salt and eggs. Mix well. Form into 1-inch balls. Place in a lightly greased baking dish. Mix apricot preserves and barbecue sauce together and pour over meatballs. Bake at 350° for 45 minutes or until nicely browned.

May be served in a chafing dish.

SAUSAGE EN CROÛTE

Betty Pince

Serves 8

1 sheet frozen puff pastry
1 pound pork sausage
½ cup chopped onion
⅓ cup chopped green pepper
1 large tomato, diced
1 cup shredded Swiss cheese
3 tablespoons chopped parsley
1 well-beaten egg

Thaw puff pastry for 20 minutes. Meanwhile, brown sausage. Add onion and green pepper and sauté 5 minutes. Remove from heat. Drain off excess drippings. Add tomato, cheese and parsley. Roll pastry into 14x10-inch rectangle. Transfer to baking sheet lined with brown paper. Spread mixture on pastry. Roll up from longest side. Pinch edges to seal. Form into circle. Slash two-thirds the way through at 1½-inch intervals. Brush with beaten egg. Bake at 425° for 20 minutes. Serve warm.

Superb hors d'oeuvre! I have also used this for brunch.

❦❧

COLD PORK LOIN SLICES

Gretchen Frazer
   1940 U.S. Olympic Ski Team
   1948 U.S. Olympic Ski Team
      Gold and Silver Medalist
Don Frazer
   1936 and 1940 U.S. Olympic Ski Team

Serves 25-30

5-6 pound pork loin, boned and tied
1 tablespoon dry mustard
1 tablespoon thyme
Toasted sesame seeds

MARINADE SAUCE
½ cup sherry
½ cup soy sauce
3 cloves garlic, minced
2 tablespoons grated fresh ginger

CURRANT SAUCE
1 (8 ounce) jar currant jelly
1 tablespoon soy sauce
2 tablespoons sherry

SPICY APPLE SAUCE
2 cups applesauce
¼ cup horseradish

MUSTARD SAUCE
2 tablespoons dry mustard
2 tablespoons boiling water
¼ teaspoon vegetable oil
⅛ teaspoon salt

SAUCES   Combine ingredients for each sauce separately and blend until smooth.

Rub roast with mixture of mustard and thyme. Marinate in MARINADE for 2 hours, turning occasionally. Roast pork at 325° for 25 minutes per pound, basting occasionally with MARINADE. Remove from oven, cover with CURRANT SAUCE and allow to cool for several hours. Slice very thin, sprinkle with sesame seeds and serve with SPICY APPLE SAUCE or MUSTARD SAUCE.

MY BROTHER-IN-LAW STEVE'S FAVORITE CHOPPED LIVERS
Carolyn Olbum

5 onions, diced
1 pound chicken livers
3 tablespoons butter
6 hard-boiled eggs
2 tablespoons rendered chicken fat
2-3 tablespoons mayonnaise
Salt and freshly ground pepper

Sauté 3 diced onions in butter until limp. Add livers and sauté until golden brown. Refrigerate to cool before grinding. Grind cooked liver with hard-boiled eggs. Add 2 diced onions, chicken fat and mayonnaise and salt and pepper to taste.

❧❧❧❧

ASPARAGUS TEMPURA
Kathi Freeman

Serves 8

2 cups ice water
1⅔ cups flour
1 egg yolk
⅛ teaspoon baking soda
3 cups oil
2 pounds thin, fresh asparagus
Salt

Combine ice water, flour, egg yolk and baking soda and beat until smooth. Cover and refrigerate until ready to use. Heat oil in shallow pan to 375°. Trim asparagus and cut into 2-inch lengths. Dip asparagus in batter and fry in batches until golden brown. Drain on paper towels, salt lightly and serve.

❧❧❧❧

CAVIAR MOUSSE
Winki McCray

Serves 30

1½ tablespoons gelatin
2 tablespoons cold water
½ cup boiling water

1 tablespoon lemon juice
1 teaspoon Worcestershire sauce
½ cup mayonnaise
2 cups sour cream
1 teaspoon dry mustard
1 tablepoon minced onion
Salt and pepper
5 hardboiled eggs, chopped
4½ ounces red or black caviar

In a small bowl soften gelatin in cold water. Add boiling water and stir until dissolved. Transfer to a large mixing bowl and add lemon juice, Worcestershire sauce, mayonnaise, sour cream, mustard and onion. Mix well. Add salt and pepper to taste. Fold in eggs, then caviar. Pour into greased 1½-quart mold. Refrigerate until firm, 2-3 hours. Unmold onto serving platter. Garnish and serve with crackers.

AUNT GRACE'S SMOKED TROUT MOUSSE

Angela Linburg

1 small smoked trout,
   skinned and fileted
1 (3 ounce) package cream cheese
1 small onion, grated, with juice
2 tablespoons lemon juice
Dash of Tabasco
Dash of Worcestershire sauce

Serves 6

Place all ingredients in mixer and mix until smooth. Let refrigerate at least 2 hours.
Serves as a spread for rye crackers or whole wheat toast. Will keep for several days.

HOT CRABMEAT SPREAD

Carol Siegel

8 ounces cream cheese, softened
1 tablespoon milk
1 (6½ ounce) can crabmeat, flaked
3 tablespoons minced green onions
½ teaspoon cream-style horseradish
Salt and freshly ground pepper
½ cup toasted sliced almonds

Serves 8-10

Combine cream cheese and milk. Mix well. Add crabmeat, onions, horseradish, salt and pepper to taste. Blend well. Spoon into an ovenproof baking dish. Sprinkle with almonds. Bake at 375° for 15 minutes or until heated through. Serve hot with crackers.

STRING FLING SMOKED SALMON PÂTÉ

Moritz Community Hospital Auxiliary

8 ounces cream cheese, softened
16 ounces pink salmon, flaked
¼ teaspoon liquid smoke
1 tablespoon lemon juice
2 teaspoons minced onion
1 teaspoon prepared horseradish
Freshly ground pepper
Chopped parsley (optional)
Chopped pecans (optional)

Makes 3 cups

Cream softened cream cheese. Add salmon, liquid smoke, lemon juice, onion and horse-radish. Blend thoroughly. Season to taste with freshly ground pepper. Garnish with chopped parsley and/or pecans, if desired. Serve with crackers.

CRAB DIP

Sara Jean Cardozo

Serves 10

8 ounces cream cheese, softened
1 (6 ounce) can crabmeat, drained
2 hardboiled eggs, chopped
⅓ cup sour cream
⅓ cup mayonnaise
⅓ cup chili sauce
Melba toast

Mix all ingredients, except melba toast, until well combined. Serve in a large bowl with melba toast on the side.

HOT ARTICHOKES

Lois and George Fisher

Serves 8-10

1 (6 ounce) can marinated artichokes
3 green onions, chopped
1 (4 ounce) can diced green chiles
½ cup mayonnaise
1 (8½ ounce) can artichokes,
    drained and chopped
2 cups grated cheddar cheese, divided
Tortilla chips or melba rounds

Reserving marinade, drain and chop artichokes. Sauté onions in 1-2 tablespoons reserved marinade until softened, but not browned. In a mixing bowl combine chiles with mayonnaise. Blend in plain and marinated artichokes and onions. Fold in 1 cup grated cheese. Spread in greased ovenproof serving dish. Bake at 350° for 10 minutes or until heated through. Sprinkle remaining cup of cheese over top and bake another 10 minutes. Serve hot with tortilla chips or melba rounds.

Can be made ahead and refrigerated. Heat before serving.

SHEEPHERDER'S BREAD AND DIP

Susan Rathke McCoy
Vera Hill

Serves 8-10

16 ounces cream cheese, softened
3 cups sour cream
1 large onion, diced
1 teaspoon Worcestershire sauce
8 slices bacon, cooked, crumbled
1 (6-inch round) sheepherder
   sourdough loaf

Combine cream cheese, sour cream, onion, Worcestershire sauce and bacon. Mix well. Slice top off sheepherder round. Set aside. Tear out enough bite sized bread pieces from center to make hollow for cream cheese mixture. Reserve bread pieces. Spoon cream cheese mixture into bread loaf. Replace top. Wrap in foil. Place on a baking sheet and bake at 250° for 2 hours. Toast reserved bread pieces and serve along with dip filled loaf.

HOT BEEF DIP

Lynn Liffick

Serves 8-10

1 (2½ ounce) jar dried beef
1 cup water
8 ounces cream cheese
¼ cup mayonnaise
2 green onions, sliced
¼ cup sour cream
½ cup grated Parmesan cheese
1 tablespoon dried parsley flakes

Shred beef. Put in water and microwave on High for 3 minutes. Drain. Combine remaining ingredients in microwave proof serving bowl. Mix well. Stir in drained beef. Microwave on High for 3 minutes or until hot. Serve immediately with crackers or raw vegetables.

BLEU-CHEESE AVOCADO DIP

Carol Dorazio

Makes about 3 cups

4 ounces bleu cheese, crumbled
1 avocado, mashed
1 tablespoon chopped green onion
2 medium tomatoes, chopped
8 drops Tabasco sauce
5 slices bacon,
    cooked, drained and crumbled
2 teaspoons lemon juice
¼ teaspoon garlic salt

Combine all ingredients and mix well. Chill. Serve with tortilla chips.

MEXICAN SALSA

Lu Ann Terry

Makes 3 cups

6 tomatillos
6 fresh jalapeno peppers, seeded
1 onion, chopped
2 teaspoons salt
2 teaspoons cumin
2 tablespoons sugar
2 cans tomatoes with juice

Peel and quarter tomatillos. Put all ingredients in food processor and chop until desired consistency.

Delicious as a dip with fresh tostadas!

SOUPS

IDAHO POTATO CHEESE SOUP

Kathleen Dacquisto

Serves 8

8-9 (medium to large) Idaho potatoes
Salt and freshly ground pepper
½ cup butter, divided
3 onions, chopped
4 tablespoons flour
1 cup milk
2 pounds processed American cheese or cheddar, shredded

Peel and dice potatoes. Place in a large saucepan. Add just enough water to cover potatoes. Bring to a boil and simmer until potatoes can be pierced easily with a fork. Remove from heat. Without draining, mash potatoes in the remaining water. Season with salt and pepper. Add 4 tablespoons of butter and stir until melted.

In a frying pan, over medium heat, sauté the onions in 2 tablespoons of butter until golden, but not browned. Remove from heat and add flour, mixing well. Add to potato mixture. Return to medium heat. Add enough milk to give mixture a good consistency. Bring to simmer. Add remaining 2 tablespoons butter and shredded cheese. Reserve some cheese for garnish. Stir constantly until butter and cheese are completely melted. Serve hot with reserved cheese as garnish.

Great with corn bread.

෬ඏ☺ ඐ෨

ORANGE MULLIGATAWNY

(Chicken Curry Soup)
Pat Davies

Makes 4 quarts

1 (3 pound) broiling or frying chicken
2 cups orange juice
2 quarts water
1 cup chopped onion
1 cup chopped celery with tops
1 cup sliced carrots
2 tomatoes, peeled, seeded and diced
2 apples, peeled, cored, and diced
4 teaspoons salt
1 teaspoon curry powder
½ cup raw rice

Cut chicken into pieces. In a 6 quart kettle bring to boil, chicken pieces, orange juice, water, onion, celery, carrots, half of the tomatoes and half of the apples. Reduce to a simmer and cook, covered, for 45 minutes. Remove from heat.

With a slotted spoon, remove chicken pieces. When cool enough to handle, remove meat from bones, discarding skin and bones. Dice meat. Return meat to the kettle along with the remaining tomatoes, apples, salt, curry powder and rice. Cover and simmer another 30 minutes, or until rice is tender. Skim excess fat, if necessary. Serve hot.

Makes a one-dish supper with homemade bread.

MAGERITSA WITH AVGOLEMONO SAUCE

Marilyn Laggis

Serves 6-8

1 lamb tripe
1 baby lamb intestine (optional)

1 baby lamb lung
1 baby lamb heart
1 baby lamb liver
Juice of 2 lemons
3 bunches scallion, diced
¼ pound butter
½ cup chopped dill
Salt and pepper
½ cup raw rice

AVGOLEMONO SAUCE
4 eggs
Juice of 2 lemons

Wash entrails and internal meats. If intestine is used, turn inside out and wash thoroughly. Scald tripe and cover with fresh salted water. Bring to boil and simmer for 40 minutes. Soak remaining meats for 30 minutes in cold water with the lemon juice. Drain and add to tripe for last 10 minutes of cooking. Strain, reserving broth and cool. Put meat through a meat grinder, using the coarse blade. Sauté scallions in butter until soft and add to meat along with the dill and salt and pepper to taste. Add broth and more water, to cover, if necessary. Bring to a boil and simmer, covered, for at least 3 hours. Add rice about 20 minutes before soup is ready to be served. Add AVGOLEMONO SAUCE according to directions.

AVGOLEMONO SAUCE   Beat eggs well and gradually beat in lemon juice. Add hot broth slowly to egg sauce, beating constantly. Return soup to heat and stir vigorously until thickened.

Soups and sauces play an important part in Greek cooking and are closely affiliated with the traditions of Greek holy days. The most famous sauce is Avgolemono, a tart, creamy sauce of eggs and lemon juice. It is an essential ingredient in the traditional Easter Soup, known as Mageritsa. At midnight of Easter morn, the Greek places his lighted Resurrection candle on his table and breaks the Lenten fast with Mageritsa, bread, cheese and eggs.

The Greek recipes that I have were given to me by my husband's mother and his aunt. They both come from the old country and learned to cook from their own mothers who, I doubt, had a measuring cup in the house. I hope I have converted their pinches and handfuls correctly.

DUCK SOUP

Margi Humphrey

Makes 4 quarts

2 wild ducks
1 large onion, chopped
1 clove garlic, minced

2 (14½ ounce) cans beef stock
1 cup diced celery
1 cup diced carrots
1 cup diced mushrooms
3 tablespoons soy sauce
1 teaspoon Heinz "57" Sauce
1 teaspoon Worcestershire sauce
2 bay leaves
3 green onions, chopped
1 cup bean sprouts

Soak ducks for 1 hour or more in a solution of ½ cup salt to 2 quarts water. Rinse ducks thoroughly. This removes "gamey" taste.

In a 6-8 quart stock pot, combine prepared ducks, onion, garlic and stock with enough water to cover ducks. Bring to a boil and simmer for 1 hour or until tender. Remove ducks from broth. Cool. When cool enough to handle, remove meat from duck carcass, discarding skin and bones. Chop coarsely.

Add celery, carrots, mushrooms, soy sauce, Heinz "57" Sauce, Worcestershire sauce and bay leaves to stock. Bring to a boil again and simmer until vegetables are crisp-tender, about 20-25 minutes. Add chopped duck meat, green onions and bean sprouts. Simmer 5 minutes or until heated through. Thin with additional water if soup is too thick. Serve hot.

❧❧❧❧❧

CREAM OF GOOSE SOUP

Fern Jones

Serves 5-6

1 goose carcass, cooked
1 large onion, chopped

5 celery tops or 1 large stalk
1½ teaspoons salt
¼ teaspoon black pepper
¼ teaspoon prepared herb seasoning
1 large carrot, cubed
4 chicken bouillon cubes
2 quarts cold water
3 tablespoons butter or margarine
3 tablespoons flour
1 cup whole milk
1 tablespoon chopped pimento

Place goose carcass in a large pot. Add onion, celery, salt, pepper, herb seasoning, carrot, bouillon cubes and water. Bring to a boil. Reduce heat. Simmer until meat can be picked from carcass. Remove from heat. Strain liquid. Reserve 3 cups of stock. Freeze remaining goose stock for future use. When cool enough to handle, remove meat from carcass, discarding skin and bones.

Melt butter in soup pot. Blend in flour and stir until mixture becomes almond-colored. Add the reserved goose stock. Stir until mixture thickens and begins to bubble. Add milk and goose meat. Stir to heat. Add pimento. Serve hot.

CURRIED PEANUT SOUP

Judith Hancock

Serves 4-6

3 tablespoons butter
1 small onion, diced

1 medium carrot, diced
1 large stalk celery, diced
1 teaspoon curry powder, or to taste
2 tablespoons whole wheat flour
4 cups vegetable or chicken stock
½ cup peanut butter
2 tablespoons catsup
2 teaspoons Worcestershire sauce
1 cup cooked brown rice
½ cup sour cream
½ cup chopped peanuts

Melt butter in a 3 quart pan over medium heat. Add onion, carrot and celery. Cook, stirring occasionally until vegetables are soft, about 10 minutes. Stir in curry powder and cook for 1 minute. Stir in flour and cook 1 more minute. Gradually stir in stock. Reduce heat, cover, and simmer for 15 minutes. Stir in peanut butter, catsup and Worcestershire sauce until smooth. Add rice and simmer, uncovered, for 5 minutes. Garnish each serving with a spoonful of sour cream and chopped peanuts.

CHLODNIK

Harriet and Jim Barnett

Serves 10-12

1 pound beets with greens, scrubbed
6 cups water
2 tablespoons lemon juice
2 tablespoons red wine vinegar
2 cups sour cream

3 teaspoons salt
1½ teaspoons sugar
1 pound shrimp, cooked, shelled
    and chopped
3 hard-boiled eggs, riced
2 cucumbers, peeled, seeded and diced
3 tablespoons minced green onions
1 lemon, thinly sliced
¼ cup chopped fresh dill
4 radishes, chopped
¼ cup chopped chives, for garnish
10-12 ice cubes, for garnish

In a large saucepan, cook beets and greens in water until tender. Drain, reserving liquid. Chop beets and greens. Place in a mixing bowl along with reserved liquid. In a separate bowl, combine lemon juice, vinegar and sour cream. Mix well. Add to beet mixture. Add salt, sugar, shrimp, eggs, cucumbers, onions, lemon, dill and radishes. Chill thoroughly. Serve in chilled bowls. Garnish each with 1 ice cube and chopped chives.

SENEGALESE

Jim and Harriet Barnett

Serves 6

¼ cup butter
2 yellow onions, chopped
3 stalks celery, chopped
2 tablespoons flour

1½ tablespoons curry powder
2¾ cups chicken broth, divided
2 tart apples, peeled and chopped
1 bay leaf
⅛ teaspoon coriander
1 cup diced, cooked chicken
1 cup light cream
Salt
Finely ground white pepper
Paprika

In a skillet over medium heat, melt butter. Sauté onions and celery until tender. Add flour and curry. Stir and cook until smooth. Put contents of skillet in a blender with 1 cup chicken broth and the apples. Blend until smooth.

Bring mixture to a boil in a saucepan with the remaining chicken broth, bay leaf and coriander. Stir and remove from heat. Stir in chicken and cream. Add salt and white pepper to taste. Refrigerate until well chilled. Serve in chilled bowls garnished with a dash of paprika.

GUMBO

Buck Levy

Serves 10-15

1½ pound andouille
1 cup oil
1 chicken (or game birds), cut up
Salt and pepper
1 cup flour

4 cups chopped onions
2 cups sliced celery
2 cups chopped green pepper
2 tablespoons minced garlic
8 cups water or chicken stock, heated
Cayenne pepper
Salt
1 cup fresh chopped parsley
1 cup chopped green onions
Filé
Cooked rice

Sauté sausage in oil, lard or bacon drippings. Remove from pot. Season and brown chicken, remove from pot. Add oil to bring up to approximately 1 cup. Make roux with oil and flour. Add onions, celery, green pepper and garlic. Cook until glaze forms on vegetables, and the vegetables are tender. Return the chicken to the pot and cook on low heat. Stir in heated water or stock gradually. Add sausage, and bring to boil. Reduce to simmer and cook for 1 hour or more. Season to taste with cayenne pepper and salt. Approximately 15 minutes before serving, add parsley and green onions.

Serve over rice. Add ¼-½ teaspoon filé to individual servings. Filé may be placed on the table for individuals to add their own.

At least once a year we have a "gumbo party" and use local game birds instead of chicken.

THE 5:30 SPECIAL

Kathleen Duffy

Serves 8

2 tablespoons margarine or vegetable oil
1 zucchini, cut into small chunks
1 medium onion, chopped
1 clove garlic, diced
5-6 large mushrooms, chopped
1 medium bell pepper, cut into pieces
1 pound extra lean ground beef
1 (15 ounce) can tomato sauce
1 (15 ounce) can dark red kidney beans
2 cups frozen corn
½ cup burgundy
½ teaspoon Worcestershire sauce
Salt and pepper to taste
Parmesan cheese, grated

In a large heavy pot sauté zucchini, onion, garlic, mushrooms and bell pepper in margarine or oil until tender. Remove from heat. In a skillet brown the beef and add to vegetables. Add remaining ingredients except Parmesan, and simmer 35 minutes. Serve with a sprinkling of Parmesan cheese.

Delicious with hot cornbread or served over a bed of rice. This recipe, like most one-dish meals, is even tastier after the ingredients have blended together. It's a great one to make ahead and freeze for later.

AUSTRIAN GOULASH

Florence Froehlich

Serves 8-10

3 pounds chuck roast
Salt and pepper
Paprika
Flour
3 tablespoons butter
1 medium onion, chopped
2 cans beef bouillon

Cut chuck roast into 2½-inch cubes. Salt and pepper lightly. Sprinkle generously with paprika on all sides. Roll the seasoned meat in flour, just enough to coat it. Sauté quickly in butter. Transfer to a heavy pot. Sauté onions, then add bouillon and meat. Cover and simmer slowly until meat is tender. Do not overcook. When meat is almost done, add thin flour and water mixture slowly to thicken the sauce to a creamy texture. Continue simmering until sauce is smooth.

Serve with rice, potatoes or dumplings. (see index).

FIVE HOUR STEW

Diane Christensen

Serves 6

3 pounds beef stew meat,
   cut into 1-inch cubes
4-6 carrots, thickly sliced
1 cup chopped celery
2 onions, sliced
6 large potatoes, quartered
2 cans beef stock
2 cans cream of celery soup
3 tablespoons instant tapioca
1 tablespoon sugar

Layer meat, carrots, celery, onion and potatoes in a large roaster. Mix beef stock and soup together until smooth. Add tapioca and sugar. Pour mixture over meat and vegetables. Cook for 5 hours with lid on starting at 350° for 1½ hours, then lower oven to 250° for 3½ hours. Do not stir.

Do not substitute bouillon cubes for beef broth.

TOMATO SOLE STEW

Aileen Denton

Serves 6-8

2 quarts water
6 pounds medium tomatoes or 2 (28 ounce)
   cans whole tomatoes, undrained
1 cup chopped whole green onions
1 clove garlic, minced
3 stalks celery, chopped

Juice of ½ lemon
1 (8 ounce) can unsalted tomato sauce
1 (14 ounce) can unsalted green beans
1 can water chestnuts,
   drained and chopped (optional)
1 medium Idaho potato, diced
1 medium zucchini, shredded
1 tablespoon salsa
⅛ teaspoon salt
⅛ teaspoon freshly ground pepper
¼ teaspoon basil
¼ teaspoon tarragon
1-1½ pounds Dover sole fillets,
   cut into pieces

In a 4-6 quart stock pot, bring water, tomatoes, onions, garlic, celery, lemon juice and tomato sauce to a boil. Reduce heat and simmer until tomatoes are tender, or if using canned tomatoes about 30 minutes. Add green beans, water chestnuts, potato, zucchini, salsa, salt, pepper, basil and tarragon. Simmer until potatoes are tender. Add sole pieces and simmer until flaky. Serve hot with heated sourdough rolls and salad.

SALADS

KOREAN SALAD
Chris DeCarufel

Serves 6-8

1 (10 ounce) package fresh spinach
8 ounces fresh bean sprouts
1 (6 ounce) can sliced water chestnuts,
    drained

4 hard cooked eggs, sliced
6 strips bacon, crisply fried and crumbled

DRESSING
1 cup vegetable oil
½ cup white vinegar
¾ cup sugar
¼ cup brown sugar
⅓ cup catsup
1 tablespoon Worcestershire sauce
1 medium onion, quartered
Dash of salt

Wash, dry and remove stems from spinach and tear into pieces. Add bean sprouts, water chestnuts, eggs and bacon and toss lightly. Add the DRESSING and toss again, gently.

DRESSING   Combine all of the dressing ingredients in a blender and run on high speed for a few seconds.

This recipe makes lots of dressing. Usually one half of the recipe is plenty unless you really like dressing.

INDIAN SPINACH SALAD
Penny Harper

Serves 6-8

¼ cup white wine vinegar
¼ cup salad oil
2 tablespoons chopped chutney
2 teaspoons sugar
¼ teaspoon salt
1½ teaspoons curry powder
1 teaspoon dry mustard
8 cups torn fresh spinach
1½ cups chopped apples
½ cup light raisins
½ cup salted peanuts
2 tablespoons sliced green onions

In a screw top jar, combine vinegar, oil, chutney, sugar, salt, curry powder and mustard. Cover, shake and chill. Place torn spinach in large, chilled bowl. Top with the rest of the ingredients. Shake dressing and pour desired amount over. Toss and serve.

This dressing is very spicy so I suggest going light and tasting. Unusual and very tasty!

SESAME SPINACH SALAD

Jerry Ann Heaney

Serves 8

2 tablespoons sesame seeds, toasted
⅓ cup vegetable oil
¼ cup lemon juice
2 tablespoons soy sauce
1 teaspoon salt
⅛ teaspoon Tabasco
¼ pound mushrooms, thinly sliced
1 (8 ounce) can sliced water chestnuts, drained
1 (10 ounce) package fresh spinach, torn

Combine sesame seeds, oil, lemon juice, soy sauce, salt and Tabasco. Mix well. Stir in mushrooms and water chestnuts. Chill. When ready to serve, toss with torn spinach.

Wonderful winter salad.

❧❦❧

GAZPACHO

Kaye Ivatts

Serves 6

2 medium tomatoes, peeled and cubed
2 cucumbers, peeled, seeded and cubed

1 green pepper, diced
1 medium zucchini, diced
1 stalk celery, diced
1 clove garlic, minced
1 small red onion, diced
1 quart tomato juice
Juice of 3 limes
Freshly ground pepper

Place all vegetables in a large jar. Add tomato juice, lime juice and freshly ground pepper. Mix. Chill well.

Serve chilled, topped with a bit of bread crumbs or serve with a slice of sourdough bread. Keeps well in refrigerator for several days.

❧❦❧

HAWAIIAN COLESLAW

Sue Bridgman

Serves 6

1 (11 ounce) can Mandarin oranges
4 cups shredded cabbage
½ teaspoon salt
¼ teaspoon ground ginger
¼ teaspoon ground nutmeg
¼ teaspoon white pepper
1 cup drained crushed pineapple
½ cup mayonnaise

Drain oranges, reserving 1 tablespoon liquid. Combine orange liquid, cabbage, salt, spices and pepper. Toss lightly. Add oranges and pineapple, tossing all with a fork. Stir in mayonnaise. Chill well before serving.

WHITE CABBAGE SALAD

Heinz Schlosser

Serves 6

1 head cabbage
5 slices bacon, diced
1 medium onion, diced
2 teaspoons caraway
1 cup white wine vinegar
¼ cup oil
Salt and pepper
Dash of sugar

Quarter cabbage, cut out the core, then shred. Place cabbage in a mixing bowl. Sauté diced bacon until crisp, add diced onion, caraway, vinegar and oil. Simmer for several minutes. Then pour over cabbage. Add salt, pepper and sugar to taste. Mix salad well and serve warm.

Serve this salad with any hearty meal.

CARROT SALAD

Mary Anne Pinkerton

Serves 8-12

3 (16 ounce) cans shoestring carrots, drained or fresh, steamed carrots
1 large red onion, chopped
1 bell pepper, chopped
¾ cup sugar
1 teaspoon salt
½ teaspoon pepper
½ cup oil
⅔ cup vinegar
1 teaspoon celery seed

Combine carrots, onion and bell pepper; set aside. In a saucepan combine sugar, salt, pepper, oil, vinegar and celery seed, and bring to a boil. Pour over carrot mixture. Let cool. Refrigerate.

This marinated salad is easy and tastes better the day after it is made. It's also pretty and good for picnics and outdoor dining.

CRANBERRY WALDORF

Jackie Baker-Turner

Serves 8-10

2 cups fresh or frozen cranberries
2 cups miniature marshmallows
¾ cups sugar
2 cups peeled, diced tart apples
½ cup broken walnuts
1 cup heavy cream, whipped

Grind cranberries and combine with marshmallows and sugar. Cover and chill overnight. Add apples and nuts. Fold in whipped cream and chill.

Perfect with roast turkey in place of cranberry sauce.

MEXICAN CHRISTMAS EVE SALAD

Ellie Lister

Serves 8

1 medium head iceberg lettuce, shredded
8 small beets, cooked
4 Rome apples
Juice of 1 lemon
4 oranges, peeled and thinly sliced
4 large bananas, thinly sliced
3 limes, peeled and thinly sliced
1 fresh pineapple, peeled, cored and sliced
    or 1 (40 ounce) can pineapple chunks
½ cup salad oil
¼ cup red wine vinegar
Salt
Seeds of 2 pomegranates
1 cup chopped salted peanuts

Peel and thinly slice cooked beets. Core and slice apples and sprinkle them with lemon juice. Put lettuce in a large, shallow bowl and arrange beets, oranges, apples, bananas, limes and pineapples over it. Mix oil and vinegar and salt to taste. Just before serving, pour over salad. Sprinkle pomegranate seeds and chopped peanuts over all.

This recipe can be expanded nicely for a crowd and is also delightful with other Mexican foods, especially chicken or turkey. Nice for a buffet, too.

☙❧

CURRIED FRUIT AND NUT SALAD

Mary Jane Atkinson

Serves 8

1 head red leaf or romaine lettuce, torn
1 cup torn fresh spinach
1 cup halved and seeded grapes
1 (11 ounce) can Mandarin orange sections
½ cup salad oil
⅓ cup wine vinegar
1 clove garlic, minced
2 tablespoons brown sugar
2 tablespoons minced chives
1 tablespoon curry powder
1 teaspoon soy sauce
¼ cup slivered almonds, toasted
1 avocado, sliced (optional)

Drain and chill Mandarin orange sections. Combine lettuce, spinach, grapes and oranges. In screw top jar, combine oil, vinegar, garlic, brown sugar, chives, curry powder and soy sauce. Pour dressing over salad, tossing lightly to coat. Garnish top of salad with toasted almonds and avocado slices if desired.

CHICKEN SALAD PRIMAVERA

Selene Isham

Makes 2 cups

2-3 cups chicken stock
Salt and freshly ground pepper
3 chicken breasts, skinned and boned
1 (10 ounce) package frozen white corn
2 red peppers
Green grapes
½ grapefruit, peeled and segmented
Honeydew or other melon, segmented
3 tablespoons chopped parsley

CURRY MAYONNAISE
3 shallots, diced
½ cup Dijon mustard
1 teaspoon dry mustard
2 tablespoons wine vinegar
3 tablespoons vegetable oil
¾ cup mayonnaise
1 tablespoon curry powder or to taste
2 tablespoons lime juice
3 tablespoons sour cream
1 tablespoon chopped chives

Boston or Bibb lettuce

Pour chicken stock into a large, heavy casserole or medium-size frying pan. Season well with salt and pepper. Heat to a slow boil, add chicken breasts and reduce heat to a very slow simmer. The stock should cover the chicken, so add a little white wine or more stock if neccessary. Poach the chicken 10 minutes, turning once. Let cool in the stock.

Place frozen corn into a pot full of boiling, salted water. Cook 60 seconds; then drain into a colander and refresh under very cold water. Cut red pepper in half; core and remove white pith. Place peppers skin side up on a cookie sheet, and roast at 450° for 10-15 minutes or until the skin feels soft but not mushy. Let cool; slice into thin julienne and sprinkle with salt and pepper.

Slice the chicken breasts into thin julienne, discarding any gristle. Arrange vegetables, thinly sliced chicken and fruit on a large plate. Sprinkle with chopped parsley and serve with CURRY MAYONNAISE, or combine chicken and vegetables in a large salad bowl. Add CURRY MAYON-NAISE and mix well. Serve garnished with fruit and lettuce.

CURRY MAYONNAISE   Place shallots, mustards and vinegar in a bowl. Add vegetable oil gradually, mixing well with a whisk. Add mayonnaise and curry powder. Mix well. Whisk in lime juice, then sour cream and chives. Refrigerate sauce several hours or overnight.

CHEZ RUSSELL'S CHINESE CHICKEN SALAD

Russel Armstrong
Chez Russell

Serves 6

1 (2-3 pound) chicken
Salt
Tamari
Salad oil
1 cup mai fun rice noodles
1 head iceberg lettuce
1 small red pepper, seeded and julienned

DRESSING
½ cup rice vinegar
½ cup vegetable oil
1 tablespoon sesame oil (roasted)
¼ cup sugar
1 teaspoon coarse black pepper
2 tablespoons Tamari

Rinse the chicken thoroughly and sprinkle the cavity with salt. Rub the skin with Tamari and roast at 375° for about 1 hour or until the juice runs clear from the cavity. Cool completely.

Heat a 3 to 4-inch deep skillet with 1½-inches of salad oil to 350°. Add mai fun noodles and cook about 15 seconds. Turn the noodles over and cook another 15 seconds. Remove immediately to drain on a clean, dry towel.

Split the lettuce in half through the core and discard the core. Cut the lettuce into a ¼-inch julienne.

Skin the chicken and pick the meat from the bones, cut into pieces about the size of the lettuce. In a large bowl, combine the chicken, lettuce and mai fun noodles. Add the DRESSING and toss gently but thoroughly. Serve at once, garnished with the red pepper julienne.

DRESSING   Combine all dressing ingredients and mix well.

COLD FISH WITH MASHED POTATO AVOCADO SALAD

Merryl Lackey

Serves 6

1 pound thick white fish
1 yellow onion, finely sliced
Juice of 2-3 lemons
Salt and pepper

MASHED POTATO SALAD
⅓ cup olive oil
⅓ cup white wine vinegar
Salt and pepper
4 cups cold cooked mashed potatoes
3-4 avocados, peeled and thinly sliced
Juice of 1 lemon

Cube fish into ¾-inch chunks. In a bowl large enough to hold fish, combine onion and lemon juice. Season with salt and pepper. Add fish. Cover, refrigerate and allow to marinate 4-6 hours, stirring occasionally.

MASHED POTATO AVOCADO SALAD Combine olive oil, wine vinegar, salt and pepper in a screw top jar. Shake well. Combine well with mashed potatoes. Line the bottom of an 8-inch pie plate with a thin layer of the avocados. Top with a thin layer of the potato mixture. Repeat 3-4 times ending with the avocados. Sprinkle with lemon juice. Serve chilled with the marinated fish.

CHARLIE THE TUNA

Charles Stuhlberg

Serves 1-2

1 (6 ounce) can water-packed tuna, drained
¼ cup mayonnaise
1 tablespoon Dijon mustard
1 small can water chestnuts, chopped
½ medium onion, chopped
1 tablespoon lemon juice
Pepper to taste

Combine tuna, mayonnaise, mustard, water chestnuts, onion and lemon juice. Season with pepper. Chill 2 hours. Serve on lettuce leaves or on bread if you can afford the calories. Eat daily if on a diet.

SALMON MOUSSE
Louise Rathke

Makes 8 cups

2½ cups clear chicken broth, divided
1 teaspoon dried tarragon
1 lemon slice
2½ envelopes unflavored gelatin
2 tablespoons minced onion

¼ cup fresh lemon juice
3-4 dashes Tabasco sauce
Salt
1 tablespoon minced fresh dill
   or 1 teaspoon dried dill
4 cups fresh salmon, cooked
   or canned salmon, drained
¾ cup mayonnaise
1 cup heavy cream
Sprays of fresh dill or watercress
Lemon twists

Pour 2 cups chicken broth into saucepan and add tarragon and lemon slice. Simmer gently for about 5 minutes. Put remaining ½ cup broth in small bowl, sprinkle with gelatin, and let stand until gelatin is softened. Remove lemon from hot broth and stir in gelatin. Season with minced onion, lemon juice, Tabasco sauce, salt, if needed, and dill. Be generous with dill and Tabasco sauce as flavor will be more bland when whipped cream is added.

Remove any skin or bones from salmon and flake. Stir into gelatin. Purée in two batches in blender until smooth. Chill until thickened, but not set. Fold in mayonnaise. Whip cream until thick and fluffy, fold in. Taste mousse and add additional lemon juice, salt or dill if needed. Turn into 8-inch ring or fish mold rinsed in cold water. Cover with plastic film and chill overnight. Unmold onto a chilled plate, and decorate with sprays of fresh dill or watercress and lemon twists.

CURRIED RICE (OR ORZO) SALAD

Connie Grabow

Serves 15-20

2 tablespoons curry powder
⅓ cup butter
6 cups chicken broth
3 cups uncooked rice or Orzo
¾ cup chopped green onions
3 tablespoons lemon juice
2 cups mayonnaise
3 tablespoons milk
1 cup frozen peas, thawed
   (omit if using Orzo)
¾ cup slivered almonds, toasted
Parsley

Sauté curry in butter. Stir in chicken broth, bring to boil. Add rice or Orzo; cover and simmer 20 minutes or until all liquid is absorbed. Stir in green onion and lemon juice. Chill thoroughly. Combine mayonnaise and milk, blend well and stir into rice mixture along with peas and almonds. Garnish with parsley.

Orzo is a marvelous rice-shaped pasta available in Greek and Italian markets in most big cities or in those with ethnic populations. It is also available in many regular markets with special ethnic sections. Excellent with meat or fowl.

❧✿❧

INDONESIAN BULGAR SALAD

Susan Henry

Serves 4-6

1 cup dry bulgar wheat
1½ cups boiling water
½ cup raisins
2 cups chopped scallions
¼ cup toasted sesame seeds
1-2 cups fresh snow peas

½ cup thinly sliced water chestnuts
1 cup bean sprouts
¼ cup toasted cashews
1 large green pepper, chopped
1 stalk celery, chopped

DRESSING
¾ cup orange juice
½ cup safflower oil
1 tablespoon sesame oil
4 tablespoons tamari sauce
2 tablespoons dry sherry
Juice of 1 lemon
3 cloves garlic, minced
2 tablespoons grated ginger

DRESSING: Combine all ingredients for dressing several hours ahead.

Pour boiling water over bulgar and let sit covered for about 20 minutes. Pour dressing over bulgar. Combine remainder of ingredients together and add to bulgar just before serving to maintain crispness.

HOT AVOCADO DRESSING

Marion Malarkey

Serves 4

4 tablespoons butter
4 tablespoons catsup
3 tablespoons hot water
2 tablespoons sugar
2 tablespoons vinegar
2 teaspoons Worcestershire sauce
Salt
Tabasco
4 slices bacon, crisply cooked and crumbled
2 ripe avocados

In the top of a double boiler mix together butter, catsup, water, sugar, vinegar and Worcestershire sauce. Season with salt and Tabasco. Add bacon. Heat thoroughly, but do not allow to boil. Serve very hot, poured into the cavities of halved avocados.

EASY CAESAR SALAD DRESSING

Pat Gwinner

Makes 1½ cups

6 anchovy fillets, drained
3 cloves garlic, crushed
2 tablespoons lemon juice
1 cup vegetable oil
1 egg

In the work bowl of a food processor, mince the anchovy fillets and garlic. Add lemon juice and oil. Process until well blended. With machine on, add egg and process 2-3 seconds.

Toss with torn Romaine. Dressing will keep for up to 5 days, covered, in the refrigerator.

CHARLOTTE FORD'S PARISIAN SALAD DRESSING
Charlotte Ford

Makes 32 ounces

3 cups extra virgin olive oil
½ cup tarragon vinegar
1 teaspoon Lawry's seasoned salt
1 teaspoon black pepper
1 tablespoon tarragon
1 tablespoon dillweed
1 tablespoon rosemary leaves
2 tablespoons Grey Poupon mustard
1 tablespoon Gulden's Spicy Brown mustard

Combine all ingredients in a blender container and mix for 5 minutes.

This recipe happens to be one I learned when I lived in Paris, and for me salad is a very important part of a meal.

FRENCH SALAD DRESSING
Jackie Loutzenheiser

Makes 1½ pints

1 cup sugar
1 can tomato soup
1 cup oil
½ cup white vinegar
⅛ teaspoon garlic powder
1 teaspoon salt
1 teaspoon dry mustard
1 teaspoon celery seed
1 teaspoon pepper

Combine all ingredients in blender and blend 5 minutes.

Entrées

WHISKEY STEAK
Scott Cumming

Serves 4

3 filets of beef, sliced very thin
2 tablespoons unsalted butter
4 green onions, sliced
½ pound mushrooms, sliced
¼ cup Irish whiskey
¼ cup strong beef stock
¼-⅓ cup whipping cream

Heat skillet to very hot. Add butter and sauté steaks quickly, about ½ minute. Remove steaks to heated platter. Add onions and mushrooms to skillet; sauté for 2 minutes. Add whiskey and beef stock and reduce by one-half over high heat. Reduce heat to medium. Add whipping cream and stir until thickened. Pour over steaks and serve.

✧✦◗│◖✦✧

MARINATED TOP ROUND STEAK
Richard Theiler
Arid Club

Serves 6-8

1 (4 pound) top round steak, 1½-inch thick
Salt and pepper
2 cups red wine
¼ cup red wine vinegar

½ teaspoon each dried rosemary, sage, thyme and coriander seeds
2 bay leaves
10 peppercorns, crushed
2 cloves garlic, minced
¼ cup each thinly sliced onions, carrots and celery
2 tablespoons thinly sliced shallots
1 clove garlic, minced
6 sprigs parsley
2 tablespoons peanut oil
½ teaspoon arrowroot or cornstarch
1 tablespoon currant jelly
2 tablespoons cognac

Sprinkle the steak on both sides with salt and pepper. Put the steak in a dish in which it fits compactly. Combine 1 cup of the wine, the vinegar, herbs, spices and garlic in a saucepan and bring to a boil. Remove from heat and let cool. Add the vegetables, garlic and parsley to the steak. Pour the spiced wine mixture and remaining wine over top. Cover and refrigerate overnight.

Remove the steak from the marinade. Strain the marinade into a saucepan. Bring to a boil and cook down until reduced to about ¾ cup. Heat the oil in a large skillet. Add the steak and cook over high heat about 3 minutes on each side until nicely seared. Continue cooking over moderately-high heat, turning occasionally, about 10 minutes longer for rare meat. Blend the arrowroot with 1 teaspoon water and stir into the reduced marinade. Simmer until thickened, then stir in the jelly. Remove the steak to a warm serving plate. Pour off the fat from the skillet. Add the cognac and ignite it. Add the sauce and stir well. Pour the sauce over the meat. Slice the meat on the diagonal and serve hot.

MINT BEEF
Brett Stuart

Serves 4

1½ pounds sirloin or flank steak
4 tablespoons sesame oil
1 cup sliced green beans
1 cup sliced green peppers
½ cup beef stock
3 teaspoons kimchee base, or equal
    parts garlic, chili, ginger
1 bunch mint leaves, chopped
Lemon juice

Cut steak into thin strips. Heat oil in large skillet and brown meat slightly. Add green beans and green peppers and cook 2 minutes. Add beef stock and kimchee base to taste. Simmer 3 minutes. Add mint leaves and sprinkle with lemon juice.

CAUTION   Kimchee base can be quite hot; add sparingly, about 3 teaspoons for medium and 5 teaspoons for hotter, then test.

TERIYAKI
Audrey Roth

Serves 6

2 pounds sirloin steak
2 teaspoons powdered ginger
2 garlic cloves, minced
1 onion, minced
2 tablespoons sugar
½ cup soy sauce
¼ cup water

Trim all fat from steak, slice thinly and cut into portion sized pieces. Combine ginger, garlic, onion, sugar, soy sauce and water. Stir over low heat until sugar dissolves, then pour over meat. Let stand 2 hours, drain. Broil for 3-5 minutes on each side.

Rice is traditionally served with Teriyaki, but you may prefer mashed potatoes or noodles.

CHARCOALED ROAST
Bert Lance

Serves 8

3 pounds rolled beef roast
Salt
Prepared mustard
Ice cream salt

Salt and cover roast with mustard. Then roll in ice cream salt. Let sit for 2 hours in refrigerator until slight crust forms. Place over charcoal fire and turn as often as needed. Cook 1 hour for rare to 1½ hours for medium-done roast. Peel off crust and slice.

MEXICAN BEEF

Elaine Martin

Serves 8-10

1 (4-5 pound) pot roast
1 tablespoon salad oil
1 onion, chopped

1 clove garlic, minced
2 (1 pound) cans tomatoes
2 (4 ounce) cans California green chiles
½ teaspoon oregano
1 teaspoon salt
¼ teaspoon pepper
4 (15 ounce) cans red kidney beans
1 small can chopped black olives
1 can green chile salsa
Green onions, chopped
Cheddar cheese, grated
Sour cream

Brown roast in oil. Remove meat and set aside. Sauté onion and garlic in oil. Place meat, onion, tomatoes, chiles, oregano, salt, pepper, kidney beans, olives and salsa in a roasting pan. Cover and bake at 350° until meat is tender, about 3 hours.

Serve with chopped green onions, grated cheddar cheese and sour cream in separate bowls. Excellent with warmed flour tortillas or rolls.

A hearty meal that can be cooked long and slowly.

BARBEQUE BEEF

Diane Kneeland

Serves 12

1 (6-7 pound) seven bone roast
2 tablespoons olive oil
1 large onion, chopped
2 cloves garlic, crushed

2 tablespoons minced parsley
1 tablespoon thyme
1 tablespoon margarine
1 tablespoon rosemary
7 whole allspices
1 (3½ ounce) bottle liquid smoke, to taste

SAUCE
2 bottles catsup
4 tablespoons prepared mustard
6 tablespoons brown sugar
4 tablespoons vinegar
2 tablespoons chili powder
Drippings

Brown roast in small amount of oil. Cover browned roast with onion, garlic, parsley, thyme, margarine, rosemary and allspices. Roast, covered, at 350° for 3½ hours or until meat falls easily from bone. Cool. Shred meat onto a large platter and cover with liquid smoke.

SAUCE   Heat all sauce ingredients in a medium saucepan. Stir together with shredded meat.

Delicious on french rolls. Super for a picnic.

BRAISED BEEF AND MUSHROOMS

Ruth Hulbert

Serves 6

1½ pounds beef, cubed (1-inch)
2 tablespoons oil

2 cups sliced mushrooms
1 clove garlic, minced
1 cup sliced onions
1 bouillon cube
1 cup water
8 ounces tomato sauce
2 tablespoons sugar
2 teaspoons Worcestershire sauce
1 teaspoon basil, oregano or marjoram
1 teaspoon salt
Freshly ground pepper

Brown meat in oil over high heat. Add remaining ingredients. Simmer 2¼-3 hours. Serve over rice.

OLD-FASHIONED MEAT PIE

Barbara Montgomery

Serves 6

1 cup sliced carrots
¾ cup chopped celery
2 cups peeled and quartered potatoes

½-1 cup stewed tomatoes
½ cup chopped onion
1 can corn or green beans
1 teaspoon oregano
Salt and pepper to taste
Pinch of garlic salt
1 pound beef, cubed
Seasoned flour
2 tablespoons oil
½ cup flour
2 cups water
Dumplings

Combine vegetables, add just enough water to cover, and simmer until tender.

Flour meat and brown in oil, adding salt, pepper and garlic salt to taste. Add ½ cup more flour and 2 cups water, and simmer, stirring constantly until meat and flour mixture have become gravy. Combine the vegetables, including the water, and gravy mixture. Bake at 325° for ½ hour. Add dumplings on top and bake at 400° for 10 minutes.

I like to use a roast or steak instead of stew meat, and prepared powdered gravy along with my own as they have some flavors I find desirable.

BEEF KABOBS IN CREAM

Ritu Shivdasani

Serves 8-10

2 pounds minced beef
2 large onions, minced
9 cloves garlic, minced
1 large piece ginger, minced
4 green chiles, diced
1½ tablespoons red pepper, or to taste
1½ tablespoons *garam masala* or allspice
1½ tablespoons coriander powder
1½ tablespoons salt
4 slices bread
3 eggs, slightly beaten
Oil for deep frying
3 cups cream
3 cups yogurt or sour cream
Fresh cilantro leaves, chopped
Red pepper
Garam masala or allspice

Put minced meat in bowl and add onions, garlic, ginger and green chiles. Add all dry spices. Soak slices of bread in water for a second, squeeze out water and add to minced meat. Add eggs. Mix thoughly for 5 minutes. Divide mixture into equal parts, and shape them into round balls. Roll them in dry flour if sticky and fry in shallow oil until golden brown. Place in baking dish. Whisk cream and yogurt together and pour over meat balls. Sprinkle with cilantro, red pepper and *garam masala*. Bake at 350° for 15-20 minutes or until a crust forms and kabobs become tender.

Serve hot with a green salad.

BAKED BEANS WITH MEATBALLS

Honorable Ralph Harding

Serves 10-12

2 (No. 2½) cans pork and beans
1 can kidney beans, drained
1 can garbanzo beans, drained
1 can green lima beans, drained
1 cup brown sugar
¼ cup molasses
2 small onions, chopped
1 cup catsup
1 tablespoon dry mustard
4-6 drops Worcestershire sauce
4 drops liquid smoke
1 pound lean ground beef
3-4 strips bacon

Mix all ingredients together except ground beef and bacon. Form ground beef into meat balls, brown and cook in frying pan. Add to the bean mixture. Top with strips of bacon and bake about 1½ hours at 325°.

HAMBURGER HEMINGWAY

Mrs. Ernest Hemingway

Serves 4

1 pound lean ground beef
1 heaping teaspoon dried sage
½ teaspoon mixed herb seasoning

½ teaspoon Accent
½ teaspoon sugar
Salt and freshly ground pepper to taste
2 spring onions, chopped
2 cloves garlic, minced
1 heaping teaspoon India relish
2 tablespoons capers
1 tablespoon parsley, minced
   or 1 teaspoon dried parsley
½ cup dry white wine
2 tablespoons oil

Break up the ground beef with a fork and thoroughly mix in the sage, herb seasoning, Accent, sugar, salt and pepper. Then mix in the onions, garlic, relish, capers, parsley and wine. Form into patties.

Heat oil in a skillet until hot but not smoking. Drop in patties and reduce heat or take pan off heat. Fry 4 minutes. Remove from burner and turn heat to high again. Flip; put back on high heat and let sizzle 1 minute. Lower heat and cook 3 minutes.

VARIATIONS:

1 cup shredded cheddar cheese; 1 clove garlic, minced; ½ cup white wine; salt and freshly ground pepper.

1 small can water chestnuts, chopped; 2 spring onions, chopped; ¼ teaspoon oregano; 2 tablespoons soy sauce; no salt.

¾ cup finely chopped mushrooms; ⅜ teaspoon marjoram; 1 tablespoon Piccalilli; ½ cup white wine; salt and freshly ground pepper.

¾ cup finely chopped walnuts; 1 teaspoon oil; 1 heaping teapoon dried dill seed; ½ cup red wine; salt and freshly ground pepper.

½ cup shredded tart apple; 1 shallot, chopped; ⅓ cup toasted and chopped almonds; ½ cup red wine.

Fat juicy patties, soft but not runny.

VEAL BIRDS FORESTIÈRE

Peggy Wayne

Serves 4

FILLING
6 ounces lean ground pork
1 clove garlic, minced
1 tablespoon chopped parsley
1 small onion, minced
1 celery stalk, minced
¼ teaspoon rosemary
¼ teaspoon crushed sage
Salt and pepper to taste
Olive oil

VEAL
12 pieces veal, sliced thin and pounded
12 (1 ounce) slices Jack cheese
¼ cup flour
4 tablespoons butter
1 tablespoon grated lemon rind
1 ounce Marsala wine
12 medium mushrooms, sliced
1 ounce white wine
½ ounce brandy
½ cup beef stock or demi-glaze
¼ cup Parmesan cheese

POLENTA
6 cups water
1 teaspoon salt
2 cups cornmeal

FILLING   Combine ingredients and sauté in small amount of olive oil until pork changes color. Cool.

VEAL   Place a piece of Jack cheese on each piece of veal. Put 1 teaspoon of the **FILLING** in the center of each piece of veal, roll the meat, and secure with wooden picks. Dredge the rolls in flour and brown them in butter. Add lemon rind. When the veal birds are browned, add Marsala and flame. Turn, add mushrooms, then wine, brandy and a little of the beef stock. Place in baking dish, cover with drippings and a little more beef stock, and finish by sprinkling with Parmesan cheese. Bake at 275° for 15 minutes. Serve in nest of **POLENTA**.

POLENTA   Bring water to a boil, add salt. Stir cornmeal in gradually and cook for about 5 minutes, stirring constantly until mixture is smooth and thick. Cook over boiling water for 30 minutes.

Everybody's Favorite Liver

Jim MacVicar

Serves 4

1 pound calves livers
½ cup flour, seasoned with
    freshly ground pepper
4 tablespoons butter
3 tablespoons chopped parsley
6 tablespoons Dijon mustard
Bread crumbs
2 tablespoons butter, melted

Coat liver with seasoned flour. Sear liver in butter for 1 minute on each side. Remove from pan. Mix parsley with mustard and blend into butter residue. Coat liver with the mustard blend and then roll liver in bread crumbs. Liver may then be stored in refrigerator on wax paper until ready to cook. Drizzle melted butter on the prepared liver and broil each side for 1-2 minutes.

Lamb Shanks

Charlie Schalk
The Tram Restaurant 1946-1960

Serves 6-8

3 tablespoons bacon fat
6-8 lamb shanks, trimmed

Salt and freshly ground pepper
2 onions, chopped
4 carrots, sliced
4 stalks celery, sliced
2 bay leaves
½ teaspoon crushed rosemary
½ teaspoon crushed thyme
½ cup water
½ cup red wine (optional)
2 tablespoons flour
Thyme and rosemary to taste

In a heavy pot with a tight lid, melt the bacon fat, then place lamb shanks in fat, rolling them to coat all sides. Brown under broiler, and turn so they are sealed on all sides. Drain off all fat and blot the shanks with paper towels to remove any remaining grease. Wipe out pot and replace shanks on a small rack.

Sprinkle shanks with salt and pepper. Cover with vegetables and herbs and add water. Cover and bake at 325° for 1½ hours at 6,000 feet or 1 hour at sea level. Open pot and move top shanks to bottom, bottom ones to top, add wine, recover and bake until fork tender. The meat should be almost falling off the bones. Remove bay leaves, pour off broth and separate fat from juice. Thicken the juice with 2 tablespoons flour. Stir and cook, adding a bit more thyme and rosemary to taste.

This can be done ahead and frozen.

BRAISED LAMB SHANKS

Leif Odmark

Serves 4

2 lamb shanks, outside fat removed
1 clove garlic, minced
¼ cup flour
½ teaspoon nutmeg

¼ teaspoon each basil, thyme
Salt and pepper, to taste
Snipped parsley (optional)
1-2 tablespoons vegetable oil
1 cup water
½ cup beef stock
½ cup red wine
1 box oxtail soup mix (Knorr)
¼ cup lemon juice
1 tablespoon lemon rind
1 bay leaf
Dash of nutmeg

Trim the fat from the shanks and rub thoroughly with the minced garlic. Mix the flour, nutmeg, basil, thyme, salt, pepper and parsley in a bowl and roll the shanks in the mixture. Brown in sizzling oil in a heavy skillet. Remove from skillet and arrange in a casserole dish. In a mixing bowl combine water, beef stock, red wine, soup mix, lemon juice, lemon rind, bay leaf, salt and pepper. Stir well and pour over lamb shanks. Sprinkle with a dash of nutmeg on top of shanks. Cover and bake at 350° for 1½ hours. Lamb shanks should be baked until the meat is almost ready to fall off the bone.

The above mixture will make its own gravy. For an extra colorful and tasty combination, add small potatoes, carrots, onions and turnips the last ½ hour of baking.

❧✿⦿❧

LUSCIOUS LAMB SHANKS

Jo Ann Boswell

Serves 4

4 lamb shanks
1 teaspoon dill
½ teaspoon oregano
1 teaspoon rosemary
1 large clove garlic, minced
1 large onion, thinly sliced
1 (8 ounce) can tomato sauce
1 cup vermouth
¼ cup brown sugar
1½ teaspoons salt
⅛ teaspoon pepper

Place lamb shanks in a roaster and add remaining ingredients. Cover roaster and bake 3 hours at 300°. If shanks are large, bake at 325°. Remove cover, and continue baking for 30 minutes. Pour sauce into saucepan, reduce to half over high heat. Pour over shanks. Higher altitude may require longer baking, until meat falls from bones.

Rivals the lamb shanks at the Christiania!

TIKKA KABOB

Gretchen Rust

Serves 4

3 dried red chile peppers, crushed
1 clove garlic, minced
1 cup crushed tomatoes
½ teaspoon garam masala
Salt and pepper to taste
4 tablespoons vinegar
4 tablespoons salad oil
1 pound lamb stew meat

Mix together the chiles, garlic, tomatoes, garam masala, salt, pepper, vinegar and oil. Marinate the lamb in this mixture for at least 1 hour. Place meat on skewers and cook over coals or broil.

This recipe is from my husband's Peace Corps experience in Pakistan.

LAMB SHANKS ROSEMARY

Dorice Taylor

Serves 4

2 tablespoons olive oil
4 lamb shanks
1 clove garlic, minced
3 tablespoons vinegar
3 tablespoons lemon juice
2 tablespoons brown sugar
⅓ cup catsup
½ cup red wine
½ teaspoon salt
¼ teaspoon pepper
1 tablespoon dried rosemary, crushed

Brown the lamb shanks well and slowly in the olive oil in a heavy skillet or electric fry pan. Bring the other ingredients to a boil in a heavy covered pot or casserole. Add the lamb shanks, and simmer covered at low temperature until fork tender, at least 3 hours. Serve with the sauce.

Ask the butcher to crack the lamb shanks. I haven't the faintest idea what this means, but that's all right because the younger butchers don't know either. Serve the lamb shanks with rice pilaf, a spiced peach to give a little color to the plate, and a tossed green salad.

When Sun Valley first opened, this was sheep country and lamb shanks were as easy to get as hamburger is today. This recipe was given to me as the original recipe used by Charlie Schalk, who first made them popular in the early days in his restaurant, the Tram, on Main Street. Charlie says it is not quite the same, but I think you will like it.

SPRING RACK OF LAMB
Edward Lind
Ore House

Serves 6

2 racks of lamb
2 cups burgundy wine
2 tablespoons diced onions
¾ teaspoon oregano
¾ teaspoon freshly ground pepper
2 tablespoons lemon juice
¾ teaspoon garlic powder
1½ teaspoons salt
¼ cup soy sauce
¼ cup Worcestershire sauce
¼ teaspoon cumin
Mint jelly

Combine the wine, onions, oregano, pepper, lemon juice, garlic powder, salt, soy sauce and Worcestershire sauce, and marinate the racks of lamb for 2 hours. Broil approximately 15-18 minutes. Sprinkle with cumin. Serve with mint jelly.

MARINATED LAMB CHOPS
Gertrude Potters

Serves 4

8 (1-inch thick) loin lamb chops, trimmed
2 tablespoons wine vinegar
1 tablespoon lemon juice
1 small onion, sliced
2 teaspoons mustard
3 tablespoons olive oil
1 clove garlic, minced
¼ teaspoon ground ginger
1 teaspoon rosemary
¼ teaspoon salt

Place lamb chops in deep ceramic or glass bowl. Combine remaining ingredients and pour over chops. Marinate in the refrigerator, covered, for 4-5 hours. Broil over a hot charcoal fire or under an oven broiler for 5 minutes per side for medium rare.

FRUIT STUFFED PORK TENDERLOIN

Angela Holvey

Serves 4

1½ pounds pork tenderloin, trimmed
1 clove minced garlic
½ teaspoon paprika
1 bay leaf
1 teaspoon thyme
1 bottle Burgundy wine
½ cup chicken stock

¼ teaspoon nutmeg
Salt and white pepper to taste
3 sprigs parsley, minced
¼ cup flour
2 tablespoons butter

STUFFING
3 tablespoons butter
¼ cup minced onions
¼ cup chopped celery
½ cup peeled and chopped apple
2 tablespoons chopped parsley
Salt and white pepper to taste
½ cup chopped apricots
½ cup chopped prunes
½ cup chopped walnuts or pecans
½ cup fresh bread crumbs
Chicken stock, to moisten

Pound tenderloin with mallet until fairly flattened. Rub with garlic, sprinkle with paprika, and place in a deep casserole dish. Add the bay leaf, thyme, wine, stock, nutmeg, salt, pepper and parsley. Cover and let stand in the refrigerator for 12-24 hours, turning occasionally.

Remove tenderloin from marinade. Strain the liquid and reserve. Dust tenderloin with flour, heat butter in a large skillet, and place tenderloin fat-side down. Cook for about 5 minutes until it is well browned. Remove and place in the oven, uncovered, and bake at 350° for 30 minutes.

Remove from oven and pour off fat. Place the tenderloin fat-side up in the baking dish, pour ½ cup of reserved liquid over it, then place the stuffing on top of flattened tenderloin, roll and secure with round toothpicks. Continue to bake, covered, for 30 minutes and uncover for the last 30 minutes of baking. Let stand at room temperature for about 15 minutes before slicing.

STUFFING   Melt the butter over moderate heat in a 8 to 10-inch skillet. Add onion and cook, stirring frequently for about 3 minutes. Add the celery and apples, cook until just limp without browning. Remove from heat and combine the remaining ingredients. Mix thoroughly.

If you desire a gravy with the tenderloin, I suggest the packaged pork flavor gravy mix. It's very tasty and less trouble.

PORK CHOPS AND LIMA BEANS

Mrs. David M. Bramble

Serves 4

4 pork chops
Salt and pepper
Dried dill
1 tablespoon flour
1 (15 ounce) can butter beans,
    liquid reserved
½ package mushroom gravy mix (optional)
½ cup water

Trim fat from chops. Cut fat into cubes. Place in a skillet and cook over medium heat until browned. Remove and set aside for another use. Brown chops in the same skillet. Transfer to a casserole dish and season with salt, pepper and dill. Pour off fat from skillet leaving 1 tablespoon. Add flour and reserved liquid from beans. Stirring well, scrape up brown bits from pan. Pour beans over chops. Pour gravy over beans. If desired, add ½ package gravy mix with ½ cup water for more gravy. Cover and bake at 325° for 1½ hours.

PORK ZUCCHINI DELIGHT

Sheila Longley

Serves 6-8

1½ pounds ground lean pork
1 clove garlic, minced
Salt and freshly ground pepper
3-4 medium zucchini, cut into strips
2 cups sour cream
1 pound Mozzarella cheese, shredded
½ cup grated Parmesan cheese
Bread crumbs

In a skillet brown meat with garlic, salt and pepper. Layer meat in a lightly-greased casserole dish alternating with zucchini strips, sour cream and Mozzarella. Top with Parmesan cheese and bread crumbs. Bake at 350° for 1 hour.

TURKEY WITH SWEET & SOUR SAUCE

Mrs. Ernest Hemingway

Serves 24

1 (10-12 pound) turkey
2 Bermuda onions, quartered
2 apples, peeled, cored and quartered
5 peaches
¾ cup white grapes
1½ teaspoons freshly grated ginger root
Juice of 4 limes
2½ cups chicken stock
5 tablespoons corn starch
2½ cups dry white wine
½ cup sugar
⅓ cup white vinegar
1 tablespoon soy sauce
Salt and freshly ground pepper to taste
1 oven cooking bag

Stuff turkey with the onions and apples. Bake in cooking bag as directed on package label. When done, cool and remove meat from bones (about 16 cups turkey meat). Meanwhile, gently poach fresh peaches and remove skins. Combine in bowl with grapes, grated ginger root, and lime juice. Marinate while turkey is roasting.

In a saucepan blend a small amount of chicken stock with the cornstarch to make a smooth paste. Gradually add remaining stock and white wine. Simmer over low heat, stirring constantly, until mixture begins to thicken. Add remaining ingredients, and cook, stirring constantly until mixture is thoroughly cooked. Drain juice from fruits, and add fruits to sauce with the cooked turkey. Turn into baking dishes. Bake at 350° about 30 minutes or until heated through. Serve with rice.

If you have any left over, freeze. It will taste even better the second time around.

꧁⦿⦿꧂

CAROL'S LEMON CHICKEN

Joanne Russell
Serves 6-8

6-8 boneless chicken breasts
1 lemon
⅓ cup flour
1½ teaspoons salt
½ teaspoon paprika
4 tablespoons oil
2 tablespoons brown sugar
1 can chicken stock
1 lemon, thinly sliced

Wash, dry and skin chicken breasts. Grate peel of 1 lemon, and squeeze juice over chicken pieces. Roll chicken in flour seasoned with salt and paprika. Brown chicken in oil. Arrange chicken in baking dish, and sprinkle with brown sugar and grated lemon peel. Pour chicken stock over all. Arrange 1 lemon slice over each piece. Cover and bake at 375° for 40-45 minutes.

SPECIAL CHICKEN

Felix Gonzales
Christiania Restaurant

Serves 2

1 double breast of chicken, boned
1-2 tablespoons olive oil
1 tablespoon minced shallots
1 teaspoon minced garlic
½ cup good quality white wine
1 tablespoon brown sauce,
   preferably homemade
Salt and pepper
Fresh asparagus spears, steamed
Lemon juice
Hollandaise sauce

Sauté shallot and garlic in oil over medium heat until transparent. Add chicken, skin side down, and brown until golden. Remove chicken. Deglaze pan with wine, scraping up any brown bits left on the bottom. Stir in brown sauce. Lower heat slightly. Return chicken to pan skin side up. Season with salt and pepper. Continue cooking until completely cooked. Arrange warm asparagus on heated serving plate. Sprinkle with lemon juice. Arrange chicken over asparagus, leaving tips showing. Pour pan juices over chicken and cover the asparagus tips with Hollandaise. Serve immediately.

DIJON CHICKEN WITH CAPERS

Patti Ahrens

Serves 4-6

3 chicken breasts
Flour
1 teaspoon rosemary
¼ cup butter
½ cup cognac
3 tablespoons chicken stock
2 tablespoons lemon juice
1 tablespoon Dijon mustard
2 tablespoons capers, drained
Salt and freshly ground pepper

Skin and bone chicken breasts and pound between 2 sheets of waxed paper. Dredge chicken in flour and rosemary. In a large skillet sauté in butter. Heat cognac and pour onto brown chicken and flame. Remove chicken to a platter and keep warm. Mix chicken stock, lemon juice and mustard, and add to liquid in pan, stirring until slightly thickened. Add capers, salt and pepper. Return chicken to pan; heat through and serve.

ROAST CHICKEN WITH BLACK PEPPER CREAM SAUCE

Debbie Reed

1 (4 pound) roasting chicken
Salt and pepper
1½ cups dry white wine
1 medium onion, chopped
1 clove garlic, minced
1 cup heavy cream
1 tablespoon crushed black peppercorns

Serves 4

Remove giblets; reserve. Rinse chicken and pat dry. Season inside and out with salt and pepper. Truss. Roast in pan with wine, onion and garlic at 350° for approximately 20 minutes per pound. Add water to cover giblets in saucepan and simmer until chicken is done. Strain roaster cooking liquid into pan and add strained giblet cooking liquid. Reduce to ¾ cup in saucepan over high heat. Bring cream and black peppercorns to a boil and stir into reduced liquid in saucepan. Cook for 5 minutes. Serve over carved chicken.

CHICKEN WITH TARRAGON

Richard Theiler
Arid Club

1 (2-2½ pound) chicken, split in half
Salt and freshly ground pepper
2 tablespoons butter
2 tablespoons shallots, minced
2 teaspoons minced fresh tarragon,
    or 1 teaspoon dried tarragon
½ cup dry white wine
¼ cup water or mild chicken stock

Serves 4

If the backbone is still attached to one of the chicken halves, hack it away or have this done by the butcher at the time of purchase. This will hasten the cooking. Reserve the backbone. Also, it is best to sever the joint that connects the thigh bones with the legs. Do not cut through but leave the thighs and legs otherwise attached.

Sprinkle the chicken with salt and pepper. Heat the butter in a heavy skillet large enough to hold the whole chicken. Add the chicken, skin side down. Surround it with the gizzard, liver, heart, neck and backbone. Cook about 10 minutes until golden brown on the skin side. Turn and cook about 5 minutes longer. Remove the chicken and set aside.

Add the shallots to the skillet and cook briefly. Add the tarragon and wine. Stir to dissolve the brown particles that cling to the bottom of the skillet. Stir in the water or stock. Return the chicken to the skillet, skin side up, and cover. Cook about 15 minutes. Uncover, and place in oven for 5 minutes or longer at 375°, basting often, until chicken is thoroughly tender and nicely glazed.

MEXICAN CHICKEN CASSEROLE

Mrs. Dick Durrance

Serves 8-10

1 small bunch celery tops
4-6 whole black peppers
½ bay leaf
2 (2½-3 pound) whole fryers
6 corn tortillas
1 can cream of mushroom soup
1 can cream of chicken soup
1 pound fresh mushrooms, sliced
1 (4 ounce) can chiles
1 small can sliced black olives
1 cup shredded sharp cheddar cheese

Bring a large kettle of water to a boil and add celery, peppers and bay leaf. Add whole chickens and simmer 30 minutes. Allow to cool and reserve stock.

Dip tortillas into chicken stock and break into pieces. Place in casserole. Remove chicken from bones and place in casserole. Mix together mushroom soup, chicken soup, mushrooms, chiles, olives and ½ cup cheese. Pour over chicken. Bake at 350° for about 30 minutes. Sprinkle with remaining ½ cup cheese and return to oven for an additional 5 minutes.

❧❦❧

COUNTRY CHICKEN PATTIES AND LETTUCE

Paula Collier

Serves 4

2 whole chicken breasts
¾ cup dried bread crumbs

3 tablespoons mayonnaise
1 tablespoon minced parsley
1 tablespoon dry sherry
2 teaspoons minced onion
¼ teaspoon pepper
1 egg
¼ cup water
Salt
¼ cup salad oil
1 medium iceberg lettuce,
    coarsely shredded
¾ cup water
1 cup frozen peas

Remove skin and bone from chicken breasts. Cut into 1-inch chunks and use food processor to coarsely grind meat. In a large bowl, mix ground chicken, bread crumbs, mayonnaise, parsley, sherry, onion, pepper, egg, ¼ cup water and ¾ teaspoon salt. Shape chicken mixture by tablespoons into 1½-inch round patties. In a 12-inch skillet, cook patties in hot oil on medium heat, a few at a time until golden. Remove and keep warm.

Add lettuce to the drippings in the skillet and cook over medium heat. Stir to coat and add ¾ cup water and ½ teaspoon salt. Cook 3 minutes, stirring frequently. Add frozen peas and cook 5 minutes.

Serve patties on lettuce and peas.

HAWAIIAN CHICKEN

Gretchen Dermody

Serves 4-6

1 large fryer, cut-up
Salt and freshly ground pepper
3 tablespoons vegetable oil
1 tablespoon cornstarch
2 tablespoons soy sauce
2 cups pineapple juice
3 tablespoon vinegar
½ cup brown sugar
½ cup pineapple chunks
1 green pepper, sliced
1 tomato, cut in wedges

Salt and pepper chicken, and fry in oil for 20 minutes, browning on both sides. Remove to baking dish. To make sauce, combine cornstarch, soy sauce, pineapple juice, vinegar and sugar. Boil until clear, about 5 minutes. Pour sauce over chicken, top with pineapple chunks, peppers and tomato wedges. Bake for 30-40 minutes at 325°.

Serve with steamed rice.

⁓〰◐◑〰⁓

SPINACH CHICKEN BURRITOS

Christin Cooper
1984 U.S. Olympic Ski Team
Silver Medalist

Serves 4-6

1 clove garlic, minced
½ cup chopped onion

2 tablespoons oil
1 cup cooked chopped spinach
1 cup cooked chicken, shredded
1 cup tofu or 2 eggs
1 (4 ounce) can diced green chiles
½ cup shredded cheddar cheese
½ cup green chile salsa,
  or hotter picante sauce
Salt and pepper to taste
½ cup crushed tortilla chips
12 flour tortillas
3 medium tomatoes, diced
Cheddar cheese, shredded
Green onions, diced
Sour cream and salsa

In medium saucepan sauté garlic and onion in oil until lightly golden. Add spinach, chicken, tofu or eggs, chiles, cheese, salsa and spices. Warm over medium heat until well blended and cheese is melted. Add tortilla chip crumbs as needed until all the extra liquid is absorbed, but not dry. Mixture should be moist but not runny enough to soak through tortilla. Fill each tortilla with ¼ cup of mixture and some diced tomatoes. Roll up and sprinkle with cheese and green onions. Broil until cheese is bubbly on top. Serve with sour cream and salsa.

Variations *Substitute Monterey Jack, Parmesan or cream cheese for cheddar.*
Add 1 diced jalapeno pepper for hotter version.

ENCHILADA VERDE

Louise Wolfinbarger

Serves 6

2 whole chicken breasts
1 cup chicken stock
6 ounces cream cheese
2 cups heavy cream

6 fresh poblanos chiles,
   or 6 large green peppers
1 egg
1½ teaspoons salt
¼ teaspoon freshly ground pepper
1 medium onion, diced
1 (10 ounce) can Mexican green tomatoes,
   drained
2 serrano chiles or 2 jalapenos
2 teaspoons fresh chopped cilantro
3 tablespoons oil
12 tortillas
¼ cup grated Parmesan cheese
⅓ cup shredded cheddar cheese

Place chicken breasts in saucepan with stock, bring to boil, reduce heat, and simmer for about 20 minutes or until tender. Remove breasts and allow to cool. When cool, remove skin and bone and shred meat.

Beat cream cheese, add ½ cup cream and beat again. When thoroughly blended, add chicken and mix well. To remove skins from peppers, place on skewer and roast over open flame or place in oven 3 inches from broiler. Allow skin to blister, then place in towel to cool. When cool, gently rub peppers with towel to remove skin. Remove membrane from inside, chop coarsely and place in blender. Blend on high with remaining 1½ cups cream, egg, salt, pepper, onions, tomatoes, jalapenos and cilantro. Add ½ cup reserved chicken stock, blend for 10 seconds until puréed. Pour into bowl.

Heat oil, dip tortillas into sauce, and sauté in oil. When you have sautéed all tortillas, place ¼ cup filling in each tortilla and roll into cylinders, placing seam down in baking dish. Pour remaining sauce over tortillas. Add Parmesan and cheddar cheeses to top. Bake until cheese is melted at 350° for 15 minutes.

Serve with a tossed salad, quick buttermilk rolls, and a glass of sangria.

❧

CHICKEN CHIP BAKE

Donna Sweasey

Serves 6

2 cups cubed cooked chicken
2 cups diced celery
¾ cup mayonnaise
2-3 tablespoons lemon juice
2 teaspoons minced onion
½ teaspoon salt
Dash of cayenne pepper
Parsley (optional)
Dill (optional)
½ cup grated cheddar cheese
1 cup crushed potato chips

Mix lightly all ingredients except cheese and potato chips and place in a casserole dish. Top with cheese, then chips. Bake at 425° for 20 minutes.

ORANGE ROUGHY FILLETS

Cathy Negreponte

Serves 4

4 Orange Roughy fillets
1 cup white wine
¼ teaspoon salt
⅛ teaspoon pepper

4 capers
6 medium mushrooms
Chopped parsley

SAUCE
3 tablespoons butter
1 tablespoon flour
2 egg yolks
½ cup cream
¼ cup fish stock
Salt and freshly ground pepper
2 teaspoons lemon juice
Chopped parsley
Lemon wedges

Put fillets in a buttered skillet. Add wine, salt, pepper and capers. Bring liquid to a boil, cover, and simmer for 10 minutes. Remove fish to a serving platter. Sauté mushrooms. Top fish with mushrooms and sprinkle with parsley. Cook remaining liquid until reduced to ½ cup.

SAUCE   In a saucepan melt butter then stir in flour, cook for 5 minutes. Stir in egg yolks mixed with cream. Strain and stir in fish stock. Season to taste with salt and pepper and add lemon juice. Pour sauce over fish on serving platter. Sprinkle with chopped parsley and garnish with lemon wedges.

SOLE ALMONDINE

Eddie and Sunny Tapper

Serves 4

6 tablespoons butter, divided
4 medium tomatoes,
   peeled, seeded, and chopped
1 clove garlic, minced
½ teaspoon dried tarragon
Salt and pepper
4 sole fillets
¼ cup slivered almonds

In 1 tablespoon butter, sauté tomatoes, garlic, tarragon, salt and pepper for 1 minute. Cover and set aside. Brown fish in 4 tablespoons butter. Sauté almonds in 1 tablespoon butter. Spoon tomato mixture onto serving platter, lay fillets over and top with hot almonds.

CRUNCHY-COATED AVO-STUFFED FISH FILLETS

Carol Horton

1 avocado, peeled and sliced
Juice of 1 lemon
1½ pounds white fish fillets
¼ cup milk
¼ cup water
½ cup finely-crushed corn chips

Serves 4-6

Dip avocado slices in lemon juice and sprinkle a little lemon juice on each fillet. Place 1 avocado slice in center of each fish fillet; roll up and secure with toothpicks.

In a bowl combine milk and water. Dip each roll in milk-water mixture, then roll in corn chip crumbs to coat thoroughly. Place in a 9x13-inch baking dish and bake at 350° for 20 minutes. Garnish with remaining avocado slices.

SPICED TANGERINE FISH

Betty Allison
Bob Allison
Former Player, Minnesota Twins

Serves 4-6

2 pounds white fish, cooked
½ pound ground pork
1 tablespoon peanut oil

1 tablespoon tangerine rind
1 tablespoon minced garlic
1 tablespoon fresh grated ginger
⅓ cup slivered onions
⅓ cup slivered carrots
⅓ cup slivered black mushrooms
1 tablespoon chili sauce
1 tablespoon sesame oil
½ teaspoon sugar
2 tablespoons oyster sauce
2 tablespoons Hoisin sauce
2 tablespoons bean sauce
2 tablespoons sherry
1 tablespoon cornstarch
2 tablespoons water

Sauté pork in peanut oil with tangerine rind, garlic and ginger. Add onions, carrots and black mushrooms. Combine chili sauce, sesame oil, sugar, oyster sauce, Hoisin sauce, bean sauce and sherry. Add to pork mixture. Thicken with cornstarch and water. Pour over cooked fish.

BAKED PIKE

Clara Spiegel

Serves 4

1 medium tomato
¼ teaspoon crushed coriander seeds
Juice of 1 lemon
½ cup olive oil

Salt and freshly ground pepper
1 tablespoon minced fresh parsley
1 tablespoon minced fresh chervil
1 tablespoon minced fresh tarragon
1 tablespoon minced fresh basil
  (dill, chives, or mint may be substituted)
1 (3-4 pound) pike
3 cloves garlic
Flour
3 tablespoons butter

Prepare tomato by peeling, discarding seeds and juice, then dicing. Combine diced tomato, coriander seeds and lemon juice in a blender. With machine running, add olive oil a drop at a time, mixing constantly until thickened. Season with salt and freshly-ground pepper to taste and whisk in the parsley, chervil, tarragon and basil.

Make 6 slits along the backbone of the pike and place a half clove garlic in each slit. Pat dry with paper towels. Sprinkle with salt and freshly-ground pepper and dip lightly in flour. Melt butter in a large skillet over medium heat until hazelnut colored. Add the fish and brown on both sides. Put it into a baking dish and bake at 400° for 10 minutes for each inch of thickness, basting often. Fillet the fish and divide it onto 4 hot serving plates. Discard the garlic. Pour the sauce into the baking dish and cook gently over direct heat, scraping up any pan bits. Spoon over the fish and pass the remainder. Serve at once.

This is as good for red snapper or other white fish as for pike. If fresh herbs are not available, substitute ¼ teaspoon dried for 1 tablespoon fresh.

❦❧

FIREWORKS SHRIMP

Phil Carvey
Le Club

Serves 1

6 large shrimp, cleaned and deveined
Peanut oil
Shredded cabbage
12 cleaned snow peas

2 cloves garlic, chopped
Chili paste to taste (crushed hot chiles
  soaked in vinegar)

SAUCE
½ cup tomato purée
⅓ cup sherry
1½ ounces oyster sauce
¾ ounce soy sauce
½ ounce red wine vinegar
½ ounce sesame oil
1½ teaspoons sugar
1½ teaspoons grated ginger

Sauté shrimp in peanut oil until three-fourths cooked. Add cabbage and snow peas and toss. Add garlic and chili paste to taste. Add 2 ounces SAUCE and reduce to desired consistency.

SAUCE   Combine all ingredients, blending well.

SHRIMP DE JONGHE
Louise McCann

Serves 8

1 cup butter, melted
1 teaspoon salt
4 cloves garlic, minced
1 cup dry bread crumbs
2 tablespoons chopped parsley
⅔ cup dry sherry
¼ teaspoon cayenne pepper
2 teaspoons paprika
2 pounds shrimp, shelled and deveined

Mix melted butter with salt, garlic, bread crumbs, parsley, sherry, cayenne pepper and paprika. Stir well to blend. Put in refrigerator until it becomes slightly set, but still pourable.

Arrange shrimp on 8 scallop shells or individual ovenproof dishes. Spread the butter mixture over shrimp, carefully covering all the shrimp. Place shells on baking sheets and bake at 375° for 30 minutes. Serve immediately.

This is an excellent first or second course for dinner, or it makes a nice luncheon entrée.

CREVETTES
Sun Valley Lodge Dining Room

Serves 1

5 raw shrimp, peeled, deveined
and butterflied
1 clove garlic, minced

2 tablespoons chopped shallots
¼ cup clarified butter
Freshly ground pepper
2 tablespoons butter
3 tablespoons bread crumbs
½ teaspoon lemon juice
1 tablespoon white wine
Dash of salt
1 teaspoon fresh chopped parsley

Sauté garlic and shallots in butter until lightly browned and add shrimp. Sauté shrimp and add black pepper. When shrimp are done add butter, bread crumbs, lemon juice, wine and salt. Serve immediately, garnished with chopped parsley, in a coquille shell.

SCALLOPS ORIENTAL
Sandy Hall

Serves 4

2 pounds sea scallops
¼ cup honey
2 teaspoons curry powder
¼ cup prepared mustard
1 teaspoon lemon juice

Line broiler pan with aluminum foil. Arrange scallops on bottom of pan. Combine honey, curry powder, mustard and lemon juice, and mix well. Brush scallops generously with curry mixture. Place broiler pan in lowest position under source of heat. Broil 10 minutes. Turn scallops, brush with curry mixture, and broil 10 minutes longer or until nicely browned.

SCALLOPS GAZPACHO
Maggi O'Connell

Serves 2-4

1 pound scallops, bite size
¼ cup lemon juice
2 large tomatoes, peeled, seeded, diced
6 scallions, chopped
1 large or 2 small cucumbers, diced
1 bunch cilantro, chopped
1 cup chopped Spanish olives
1 tablespoon oil
1 (7 ounce) can salsa
1 tablespoon green taco sauce
Salt and pepper to taste

Drop scallops into boiling water, stir until they are white, about 30-60 seconds. Drain and rinse in cold water. Cover with lemon juice. Cover and refrigerate at least 1 hour. Mix all other ingredients and blend with scallops a few hours before serving. Keep chilled until serving time.

Better the second day!!

SCALLOPS EN BROCHETTE
Donna Alfs

Serves 4-6

1 medium onion
2 medium green peppers
2-3 bananas
1 (16 ounce) can pineapple chunks
1 basket cherry tomatoes
18 small or medium mushroom caps
1 (16 ounce) bottle oil/vinegar salad dressing
1 pound sea scallops

Cut up onion and green peppers in chunks of approximately 1¼ to 1½-inch squares. Slice bananas approximately ¼-inch thick. Marinate all fruits and vegetables in salad dressing for about 2 hours. Marinate scallops for only 45-60 minutes and no longer as they will lose their firmess and will not stay on skewers. Fill skewers by alternating ingredients. Save marinade for basting. Cook over medium charcoal fire for approximately 10 minutes, turning and basting frequently.

Great over rice. An especially good, light and healthful summer dish. Easy.

SEAFOOD FLORENTINE

**Bill and Jack Lennon
River Street Retreat**

Serves 4

3 tablespoons cornstarch
1¾ cups milk

⅓ cup sherry
2 tablespoons butter
½ teaspoon salt
Pinch of freshly ground pepper
1½ cups shredded Monterey Jack cheese
1 cup scallops
1 cup Snow or Dungeness crabmeat
1 cup bay shrimp
1 (10 ounce) package frozen,
 chopped spinach
Seasoned bread crumbs
1 cup shredded cheddar cheese
Chopped parsley for garnish

Stir the cornstarch into the milk to make a smooth paste. Combine with the sherry, butter, salt and pepper in a saucepan over medium heat, whisking constantly until the mixture thickens. Do not allow to boil. Remove from heat and stir in the Jack cheese, mixing thoroughly until melted.

Place the scallops in a steamer over boiling salted water. Cover and steam until just firm, not more than 5 minutes. Drain and add to the cheese sauce, along with the crabmeat and shrimp.

Prepare the spinach according to package directions. Divide among 4 individual casserole dishes. Portion the seafood over the spinach, with sauce to cover. Sprinkle with seasoned bread crumbs and cover with shredded cheddar cheese. Bake at 350° for 20 minutes. Remove from oven, garnish with chopped parsley, and serve.

❧✺◗✺❧

HOT CRABMEAT DIPPING SAUCE

Kelly G. Pandapas

8 ounces cream cheese
3 tablespoons mayonnaise
3 tablespoons dry vermouth
1 teaspoon Dijon mustard
¼ teaspoon salt
1 (7¾ ounce) can crabmeat,
 or 8 ounces mock crabmeat
Toast points

In the top of a double boiler set over hot water or very low heat, combine cream cheese, mayonnaise, vermouth, mustard and salt. Cook over simmering water until it is well-blended and heated through. Add drained crabmeat. Transfer mixture to a small chafing dish and keep hot over low heat. Serve with toast points.

Can also be used for omelette fillings, crêpes, and stuffed mushrooms.

GREEN PEPPER PIMENTO RELISH

Gail Henry
Jo Tropea

Serves 4-6

15-18 fresh green bell peppers,
    or 6 (7 ounce) cans whole green chiles
3 small cans pimentos
⅓ cup olive oil
1 tablespoon wine vinegar
1 teaspoon sugar
1 clove garlic, minced
Salt, black pepper, paprika, oregano,
    basil to taste
Dash of Worcestershire sauce

If fresh green bell peppers are used, wash and dry thoroughly. Place bell peppers on cookie sheet and bake at 400° until slightly browned. Keep turning. Remove from oven and place in brown paper bag for about 15 minutes. Remove from bag and peel, removing core and seeds. Cut into serving pieces. Drain pimentos, remove seeds and cut into serving pieces. Place in large bowl, add oil, vinegar, sugar, garlic, spices and Worcestershire sauce and toss well. Cover and refrigerate about 4 hours. Toss again before serving. When using the canned chiles, drain, remove seeds and veins down the middle, and shred into serving pieces. Add rest of ingredients and proceed with recipe.

MARINADE FOR BUTTERFLIED LEG OF LAMB

Leslie and Michael Engl

Makes 2 cups

¼ cup vinegar
½ cup water
2 tablespoons sugar
1 tablespoon mustard
½ teaspoon freshly ground pepper
1½ teaspoons salt
¼ teaspoon cayenne
1 thick slice of lemon
1 slice of onion
¼ cup butter
½ cup catsup
2 tablespoons Worcestershire sauce
¼ teaspoon liquid smoke

Simmer all ingredients, except catsup, Worcestershire sauce and liquid smoke for 20 minutes. Add catsup, Worcestershire sauce and liquid smoke. Marinate butterflied leg of lamb overnight.

BARBEQUE SAUCE FOR RIBS

Sue Wolford

1 cup catsup
1 cup brown sugar
½ cup soy sauce
1 (5 ounce) bottle Worcestershire sauce
½ bottle garlic oil
1 (10½ ounce) bottle Heinz "57" sauce
1 teaspoon dry mustard
1 teaspoon ginger
Several drops liquid smoke

Combine all ingredients in a saucepan and simmer for 10 minutes. Makes enough for 15 pounds of ribs.

Excellent on chicken as well as ribs. Refrigerate leftover sauce for future use.

❧❦

MARINARA SAUCE

Carol Harlig

Makes about 2¾ cups

2½ cups imported canned tomatoes
2 tablespoons olive oil
1 tablespoon minced garlic
¼ cup tomato paste
1 teaspoon dried oregano
Salt, if desired
Freshly ground pepper
¼ cup minced fresh parsley

Purée the tomatoes. Heat the oil in a saucepan and add garlic. Cook briefly without browning. Add tomatoes, tomato paste, oregano, salt and pepper to taste. Bring to a boil and simmer 20 minutes. Stir in parsley.

❧❦

MUSTARD DILL SAUCE

Le Purrer

Makes 2½ cups

½ cup sugar
1 cup fresh dill, chopped very fine
1 cup Dijon mustard
⅓ cup wine vinegar
½ cup mayonnaise
2 tablespoons vegetable oil

Combine all ingredients except oil in a blender or food processor. Blend until mixture is smooth. While blender is still running, add oil, drop by drop, until absorbed. Store covered in refrigerator. Will keep for 1 week. Serve with fish and shrimp. Excellent with fish pâté.

The dill weed makes it very pleasing to the eye.

WILD GAME
AND
TROUT

MARIA'S GOULASH

Maria Schenkel

Serves 8

3 pounds elk, veal or beef,
  cut into 1-inch cubes
Bacon fat or oil
2½ cups chopped onions
3 tomatoes, chopped
1 bay leaf
1 cup water
Salt and pepper
4 tablespoons flour
4 tablespoons water
1 cup sliced mushrooms, sautéed (optional)
1 tablespoon Kitchen Bouquet (optional)

In a skillet brown meat in bacon fat or oil. Drain; set aside. Brown onions in same skillet. Set aside. In a dutch oven over medium heat, bring meat, onions, tomatoes, bay leaf and water to a boil. Season with salt and pepper. Reduce heat to simmer, and cook for 3 hours until meat is very tender. Pour off liquid and degrease stock. Return to dutch oven. Mix together the flour and water. Stir into goulash. Cook 5 minutes over medium heat. Add mushrooms, then Kitchen Bouquet, if desired, to darken stock.

Serve with dumplings or noodles.

DEER/ELK SAUERBRATEN ROAST

Fred Judd

Serves 6

1 (3 pound) deer or elk roast
3 tablespoons oil
½ cup brown sugar
½ cup white vinegar
2 lemon slices
2 bay leaves
1 tablespoon allspice
Salt and freshly ground pepper
1 yellow onion, chopped
1 cup water
Flour

Brown meat in oil in a heavy skillet over high heat. Place meat in crock pot and cover with brown sugar, vinegar, lemon slices, bay leaves, allspice, salt, pepper, onion and water. Cook overnight or all day on Low. Strain liquid into saucepan and add enough flour thinned with water to make gravy.

Serve meat on egg noodles with gravy on top. "Ummm."

MISSOURI GOOSE

Bill Mason

Serves 4-8

1-2 (6-10 pound) geese
1 apple, sliced

1 carrot, sliced
1 celery stalk, sliced
1 onion, sliced
10-12 juniper berries,
   or 1 ounce gin
1 cup red wine vinegar
¼-¾ jar red currant jelly
4-6 cups brown stock
Salt and pepper

Soak birds overnight in salt water. In a large pot combine apple, carrot, celery, onion, juniper berries, red wine vinegar, jelly and brown stock. Bring to a boil over medium heat. At the same time, salt and pepper geese, and brown in oven at 500° for approximately 20 minutes. Remove birds from the oven and place breast side down in the sauce. Place in a 325° oven and cook slowly for 3 hours. Allow the sauce to boil slightly. Remove birds to cool. Strain sauce and reduce for thickness. Cut geese into serving pieces and pour sauce over the carved meat.

Serve with baked apples, brown and wild rice and a green vegetable. This recipe is great also for ducks and quail.

❦❧❦

DUCKS À LA TRADER VIC

Barbara Bailey

Serves 4-6

2 whole ducks
Soy sauce, to cover
Salt and pepper

SAUCE
4 tablespoons butter
½ jar currant jelly
1 orange rind, grated
Sherry to taste
1 tablespoon cornstarch (optional)
2 tablespoons cold water (optional)

Soak ducks in soy sauce for half a day. Pat dry and season with salt and pepper. Roast at 550° according to the size of the ducks:

Extra large	30-31 minutes
Large (Mallards, etc)	28-29 "
Medium	25-27 "
Small	18-20 "

Roast a few minutes longer if the ducks are too rare for your taste. Pour SAUCE over ducks and serve.

SAUCE In the top of a double boiler, melt together the butter, jelly, and orange rind. Season to taste with sherry. If desired, thicken the sauce with cornstarch and water.

GAME BIRDS HUNTER'S STYLE

Le Purrer

Serves 4-6

3 tablespoons olive oil
1-2 game birds (or chicken), cut up

1 medium onion, chopped
2 bay leaves
2 garlic cloves, halved
2 tablespoons minced fresh parsley
1 teaspoon salt
Pinch of red pepper (optional)
½ cup dry white wine
¾ cup canned, peeled tomatoes,
    undrained
1 cup sliced fresh mushrooms
Chopped fresh parsley

Heat olive oil in skillet; sauté birds until golden. Add onion, bay leaves, garlic, parsley, salt and red pepper to pan. Simmer covered for 15 minutes. Add wine, and simmer for 15 minutes, covered. Crush tomatoes and add with the juice. Simmer about 30 minutes. Add mushrooms; simmer 10 minutes covered. Serve on a heated platter. Top with chopped parsley.

I like to prepare this early in the day. Then place in a heavy, covered oven pan. Let it blend and cool. Then place in a 350° oven until just hot and bubbly. Serve with mashed potatoes, green beans and sliced melon for dessert. This is a wonderful way to cook game birds as they are never dry.

COPPER BASIN GAME BIRDS

Kitty Willard

Serves 2

1-2 game birds
Flour seasoned with
    salt and freshly ground pepper
1½ tablespoons butter
2 tablespoons chopped shallots
¾ cup chicken stock
2 tablespoons white wine
1 (⅞ ounce) package Bearnaise sauce mix
¼ cup cream
2 tablespoons chopped fresh parsley
1 teaspoon fresh tarragon,
    or ½ teaspoon dried

Pound breast meat and tender parts of leg meat until thin. Lightly dust with seasoned flour. Sauté in butter just until golden brown. Remove to platter and keep warm. In same pan, sauté shallots until soft. Add chicken stock, wine and Bearnaise sauce mix. Simmer about 2 minutes or until smooth. Add more chicken stock if sauce is too thick. Add cream, parsley and tarragon, and heat until sauce is hot. Do not boil. Spoon over birds on a bed of rice.

Excellent for chukar, blue grouse, Hungarian partridge, pheasant, and even chicken.

STUFFED PHEASANT
Christina Potters

Serves 2-4

2 tablespoons shallots
6 ounces mushrooms, chopped
1 tablespoon walnuts
1 tablespoon parsley
Salt and pepper
1 tablespoon cognac

A brace of pheasants (2),
  dressed but not trussed
2 slices pork fat
½ tablespoon flour
2 tablespoons Madeira

STUFFING
3 tablespoons butter
6 ounces chicken livers

STUFFING   Melt 2 tablespoons butter in a large skillet and cook chicken livers gently until they begin to brown. Remove from pan and allow to cool. Melt remaining tablespoon butter in same pan. Add shallots and cook until golden. Add the mushrooms and cook 1-2 minutes. Chop chicken livers finely. Add mushroom mixture, walnuts, parsley and salt and pepper to taste. Moisten with cognac.

Fill pheasants with STUFFING and close the openings with toothpicks. Tie pieces of pork fat to each breast and place pheasants breast side down in a shallow roasting pan, resting their legs on the side of the pan. Smear backs with butter. Add 2 tablespoons water to pan. Roast pheasants at 400° for 30 minutes. Reduce oven temperature to 350° and turn birds breast side up. Cook for an additional 20 minutes basting often. Remove pork fat, baste again and let skin brown slightly for 10 minutes. The total cooking time for an average pheasant is 1 hour.

Place birds in a serving dish and keep warm. Pour off most of the fat that has accumulated in the pan. Sprinkle in ½ tablespoon flour and stir over bottom of the pan. Add 1-2 tablespoons water if juices are insufficient. Add Madeira and simmer 1-2 minutes. Taste for seasoning. Pour into sauce boat and serve.

◦✲☙◖◗❧✲◦

PHEASANT MADEIRA
Gertrude Potters

Serves 6

6 pheasant breasts
½ cup cream
Flour
Salt and paprika
½ cup butter
1 cup Madeira
½ cup sliced green grapes
1 (6 ounce) can artichoke hearts

Remove skin from breasts. Dip in cream and dredge in flour, salt and paprika. Sauté lightly in butter. Add wine and cover with foil. Bake at 325° for 1 hour and 15 minutes or until tender. Remove breasts from baking dish and set aside. Add ½ cup cream to the sauce remaining in baking dish. Reheat. Stir in grapes and artichoke hearts. Pour over pheasant and serve with wild rice.

PHEASANT AND SAGE GROUSE SAUTÉ

Doug Bell

Serves 2-4

1 pheasant breast
1 sage grouse breast
3 tablespoons salt
5-6 quarts water
Cornmeal coating mix
Pepper
8 tablespoons butter
2 stalks celery, chopped
1½ medium onions, chopped
1 cup good quality white wine
Toast points

Submerge breasts in a solution of salt and water, and soak overnight at room temperature. Bone and cut into 1½-inch cubes. Allow meat to dry for 10 minutes. Dust with coating mix and season with pepper.

In a large skillet melt butter over medium heat. Add meat and brown. Remove and set aside. Sauté celery and onion until transparent. Return meat to pan. Turn heat to high. As mixture begins to boil, add wine and boil 30 seconds more. Lower heat to simmer, cover, and cook 20-25 minutes. Serve on toast points.

PHEASANT BENJAMIN

Willis B. Benjamin

Serves 4

1 tablespoon butter
2 pheasant, cut up

Flour, seasoned with salt, pepper, parprika
1 cup chicken stock
⅔ cup vermouth
1 tablespoon butter
1 cup beef stock
2 cups whipping cream
Salt and pepper to taste
Lemon juice to taste
1 tablespoon cornstarch
2 tablespoons cold water

Melt 1 tablespoon butter in frying pan. Lightly coat pheasant in seasoned flour and brown in butter. Add chicken stock and ⅓ cup vermouth. Cover and simmer 20 minutes. In another pan melt butter, add beef stock and bring to a boil. Add cream, ⅓ cup vermouth, salt, pepper and lemon juice to taste. Bring to boil. Add cornstarch dissolved in cold water and cook until thickened. Pour sauce over pheasant and serve hot.

SWEET AND SOUR PHEASANT

Linda Vinagre

Serves 6

MARINADE
¼ cup soy sauce
1 tablespoon sherry
2 teaspoons sugar
⅛ teaspoon salt
2 small garlic cloves, minced

2 pounds pheasant breasts,
　boned and cubed (1-inch)

¾ cup flour
⅓ cup butter
⅓ cup oil
2 celery stalks, sliced
1 green pepper, cut into triangles
1 onion, cut into triangles
⅔ cup pineapple juice
1 tablespoon arrowroot
1 (20 ounce) can pineapple chunks,
　or fresh pineapple

SWEET AND SOUR SAUCE
¼ cup brown sugar
1 tablespoon cornstarch
¼ cup vinegar
¾ cup pineapple juice
1 tablespoon soy sauce
1 teaspoon Worcestershire sauce

MARINADE　Combine all ingredients.

Marinate pheasant for 1 hour in marinade. Drain. Coat pheasant pieces in flour. In a wok or large skillet, melt butter and oil and sauté pheasant until lightly browned. Remove from pan. Keep hot. Sauté celery, green pepper and onion. Mix pineapple juice, arrowroot and ⅓ cup SWEET AND SOUR SAUCE (remaining sauce may be used in another dish). Add to vegetables. Stir until thickened and clear. Add pineapple chunks and pheasant. Heat through and serve.

SWEET AND SOUR SAUCE　Combine all ingredients and cook over medium heat, stirring constantly, until sauce thickens and becomes clear.

Serve over steamed rice.

Idaho Trout Chinese Style

Don Bemco Bennett

Serves 4

4 small or 2 medium trout
½ teaspoon salt

2 tablespoons Chinese rice wine
1 tablespoon shredded, fresh ginger root
2 large scallions,
    shredded into 2-inch lengths
2 tablespoons peanut or vegetable oil

DIP SAUCE
1 teaspoon white vinegar
2 tablespoons light soy sauce
1 teaspoon shredded fresh ginger root

Clean, rinse and dry fish, leaving heads and tails on. Make 3-4 diagonal slashes on each side. Dissolve salt in wine, rub this liquid on inside and outside of fish. Scatter shredded ginger on top. Place fish on either a heat-proof dish or piece of cheesecloth on the rack of a bamboo steamer. In a large pot or kettle the same diameter as the steamer, bring water to a boil. Water should be about 1 inch below the steamer rack. Turn heat to medium-high, place covered steamer over the boiling water and steam fish for 15-20 minutes. Add more boiling water during steaming if necessary to avoid pot boiling dry.

While fish is steaming, heat the oil in a small saucepan to very hot, but not smoking. Just before serving, scatter scallions on top of fish and drizzle hot oil over fish and scallions. Watch out for hot oil spatters.

DIP SAUCE   Mix all ingredients together. Serve with trout, in individual small cups or dishes on the side.

Where do you catch the trout? Try Big or Little Wood River, Trail Creek, Warm Springs or any of the mountain lakes around Sun Valley. If the trout prove elusive, substitute fillets of red snapper, turbot, sole or other white fish.

If you do not have rice wine on hand, dry sherry is an excellent substitute. Use dark soy sauce if you do not have light. A bamboo steamer works best. The Chinese spent a couple thousand years perfecting it, but you can improvise. A large covered kettle with a cake rack or inverted dish to keep the fish above the boiling water works okay. Many woks come with a steamer rack, or use an old Chinese trick—4 crossed chopsticks.

This dish goes well with fried rice, stir-fried vegetables, various noodle dishes, etc. If you are fortunate enough to find some Tsing Tao or other Chinese beer, you have the perfect accompaniment to a meal fit for an emperor—a superb blend of Far East with Far West.

DUDE CAIN TROUT

Dude Cain

Serves 1

1 trout, cleaned
1 tablespoon dried onion
3 tablespoons minced fresh parsley
1 teaspoon Spike
    (vegetable seasoning powder)
Lemon wedges

In a pan large enough to accommodate a steam rack above 1-2 inches water, bring to a boil water, dried onion, parsley and vegetable seasoning powder. Reduce heat to a low boil. Place steam rack in pan and lay cleaned trout on rack. Cover pan. Steam 10-15 minutes, depending upon the amount and thickness of trout. Fish will flake easily when tested with a fork. Split fish in the pan, taking just the fillets, leaving skin, head, bones, etc., to be disposed of easily. Squeeze lemon over fillets.

Serve with mayonnaise, sour cream, yogurt or horseradish dressing. Excellent cold.

The only way Dude Cain will eat trout!

WARM SPRINGS FRIED TROUT

Bert Bender
Warm Springs Restaurant

Serves 4

4 (8-10 ounce) rainbow trout, gutted
Salt and pepper
Granulated garlic
1 cup milk
1 cup buttermilk
Flour for dredging
Cottonseed oil for deep-frying
Clarified butter
Lemon wedges

Wash the trout thoroughly and pat dry. Sprinkle lightly with salt, pepper and garlic. Combine the milk and buttermilk in a bowl wide enough to accommodate the trout. Dip the fish in the milk mixture, making sure that they are well moistened, then roll in the flour. Place on wax paper in the refrigerator for 1 hour. Preheat enough oil to cover the fish to 375° in a deep skillet. Cook the fish about 2 minutes per side, drain on paper towels. Serve immediately with clarified butter and lemon wedges.

CAMPFIRE TROUT
Bill Mason

Serves 1

2 fresh trout, cleaned and dressed
Flour
1 tablespoon dill
½ teaspoon basil
Salt and pepper
1 tablespoon butter
2 tablespoons white wine
1 tablespoon lemon juice

Combine flour, dill, basil, salt and pepper in either plastic bags or bowl. Roll trout, covering thoroughly in mixture. Heat large skillet over campfire. Melt butter and add white wine. Fry trout until golden brown. As trout fry, squeeze lemon juice over trout. Serve quickly.

❧❧❧

BAKED TROUT
Hildegard Raeber

Serves 1

1 trout, washed and dried
1 tablespoon butter
Salt and pepper
¼ teaspoon each fresh parsley,
   chives, dill, tarragon
1 sliver prosciutto or lean bacon
1 cup dry white wine
½ cup sour cream

Generously butter an ovenproof dish. Stuff trout with butter kneaded with salt, pepper, parsley, chives, dill and tarragon. Wrap fish with thinly sliced prosciutto or lean bacon and place on buttered dish. Add a cup of dry white wine and bake at 425° for 20 mintutes. Pour liquid into a bowl and blend well with sour cream. Pour over fish and return to oven until sauce is hot.

Serve 1 trout per person with parsley potatoes and a green salad.

❧❧❧

MICROWAVED TROUT
Sue Jacobsen

Serves 1

1 fresh trout, 8 to 10-inches
½ lemon, sliced paper thin
Lemon wedges

Rinse the trout thoroughly in cold water and place on a plate. Cover with paper thin slices of lemon and pop into the microwave oven. Cook on High for 2 minutes, turn trout over, transfer the lemon slices, and cook 1 minute more. The flesh should be just firm to the touch to be easily boned, then reheated for no more that 30 seconds and served with lemon wedges to enhance the flavor.

To me there is no finer meal than fresh trout, and this method of cooking allows the delicate flavor to be appreciated.

POACHED STEELHEAD WITH ASPIC

Claire Casey

Serves 10 depending on size of steelhead

1 steelhead, cleaned
2 quarts water
2-3 cups white wine
12-14 crushed peppercorns
2 lemons, sliced
4 tablespoons tarragon

ASPIC
Poaching water
1 egg white, slightly beaten
3 packages unflavored gelatin
1 cup cold water
Fresh dill
Radishes, sliced
Cucumber, sliced
Cocktail onions
Parsley for garnish

In a fish poacher, combine water, wine, peppercorns, lemons and tarragon and bring to a boil. Wrap whole fish in cheesecloth and lower into boiling water. Poach 10 minutes per pound at simmer. After fish is poached, remove water and save poaching liquid for ASPIC. Remove cheesecloth carefully. Chill fish.

ASPIC   Strain poaching water and bring to boil. Reduce for 30-40 minutes. Add 1 egg white. Bring to boil again. Cook for 2 mintues. Strain again through coffee type filters. This takes about 1 hour until liquid is very clear. Dissolve 3 packages of gelatin in 1 cup of cold water. Add to poaching liquid, and heat to dissolve completely. Chill liquid until it has almost set.

Meanwhile, decorate fish with dill sprigs, radishes, cucumbers or any other colorful garnish. Put a cocktail onion in the eye. As ASPIC sets, spoon over chilled fish several times until ASPIC is all used. After ASPIC sets, remove excess from around fish, add parsley or any other greens around fish, chill and serve.

The steelhead may be poached the day before. Make the ASPIC in the morning, and chill until ready to serve!

VEGETABLES
AND
SIDE DISHES

Carrot Soufflé

Cicely Nicolai

Serves 8

2 cups carrots, cooked and puréed
2 teaspoons lemon juice

2 tablespoons minced onion
½ cup softened butter
¼ cup sugar
1 tablespoon flour
1 teaspoon salt
¼ teaspoon cinnamon
1 cup milk
3 eggs

Place all ingredients in a food processor and blend until smooth. Pour into lightly buttered 2 quart soufflé dish or casserole. Bake, uncovered, at 350° for 45-60 minutes until center is firm to touch.

❦

Marinated Carrots

Dana Gunn

Serves 6-8

2 pounds carrots
1 large green pepper, chopped
1 large sweet onion, chopped
1 cup sugar
½ cup oil
½ cup vinegar
½ teaspoon salt
½ teaspoon freshly ground pepper
½ teaspoon dry mustard
1 cup tomato soup, undiluted

Slice carrots and steam lightly, retaining crispness. Layer carrots, pepper and onion in a 9x13-inch dish. In a saucepan, combine remaining ingredients and bring to a boil. Pour over carrot layers. Serve hot.

❦

Celery au Gratin

Maria Primus

Serves 4-6

2 tablespoons butter
2 tablespoons flour
1 cup chicken stock
¼ cup light cream
Salt and freshly ground pepper to taste
2 cups sliced celery, parboiled
¼ cup chopped blanched almonds
½ cup shredded cheddar cheese
½ cup bread crumbs

Melt butter in saucepan. Slowly add flour to melted butter. Remove pan from heat and slowly add stock and cream, stirring constantly. Salt and pepper to taste. Stir in celery and chopped almonds. Pour celery mixture into buttered, shallow 1½ quart casserole. Top with cheese and bread crumbs. Bake at 350° until cheese melts and ingredients are heated through.

CORN CASSEROLE

Linda Laird

Serves 6-8

½ cup butter, melted
¾ cup chopped green pepper
1 clove garlic, minced
¼ cup flour

⅔ cup milk
¾ teaspoon salt
⅛ teaspoon pepper
⅛ teaspoon basil
⅛ teaspoon oregano
¼ teaspoon sugar
1 cup shredded cheddar cheese
1 cup solid pack tomatoes, drained
9 ounces frozen corn, thawed
1 (32 ounce) can whole onions, drained

Sauté green pepper and garlic in butter. Stir in flour until moistened. Add milk, salt, pepper, basil, oregano and sugar. Heat and stir until sauce starts to thicken. Remove from heat and stir in ½ cup shredded cheddar cheese. Add tomatoes. Heat gently until mixture thickens. Pour into 2 quart casserole. Stir in corn and onions. Sprinkle with remaining ½ cup cheese. Bake at 350°, uncovered, for 50 minutes.

COUNTRY CORN PUDDING

D.J. Cahen

Serves 8

¼ cup butter
3 tabespoons flour
1½ cups milk or half & half
2 eggs
1 tablespoon chopped fresh parsley
1 teaspoon salt
¼ teaspoon ground red pepper
3 cups corn kernels, cooked
Crumbled cooked bacon or cubed ham

Melt butter in a small skillet over medium-high heat. Add flour and stir until smooth. Cook 1 minute, stirring constantly. Gradually add milk, stirring constantly, until sauce is thick.

In a large bowl beat eggs. Gradually whisk sauce into eggs, blending well. Mix in parsley, salt and red pepper. Add corn and mix thoroughly. Pour into buttered 2 quart baking dish. Sprinkle with bacon or ham. Bake at 350° for 20-30 minutes or until pudding is golden and center set.

SCALLOPED IDAHO POTATO AND ONION CASSEROLE

Governor John Evans
First Lady Lola Evans

Serves 8-10

3 pounds potatoes,
   peeled and thinly sliced
3 cups thinly sliced onions
Boiling water
2 teaspoons salt
3 tablespoons butter
2 tablespoons flour
⅛ teaspoon freshly ground pepper
⅛ teaspoon paprika
1½ teaspoon salt
2¼ cups milk
Chopped parsley

Place potatoes and onions in a large saucepan. Cover with boiling water, add 2 teaspoons salt. Cook, covered, 5 minutes or until slightly tender, then drain. Melt butter in a small saucepan, stir in flour, pepper, paprika and 1½ teaspoons salt to make a smooth paste. Gradually stir in milk. Bring to boil, reduce heat and simmer 1 minute. In greased 2 quart casserole, layer one-third potato and onion mixture, sprinkle with parsley and top with one-third sauce. Repeat, ending with sauce. Bake, uncovered, at 400° for 35 minutes.

CALIFORNIA SWEET POTATOES

Theresa Alden

Serves 4

4 sweet potatoes, or yams
¼ cup brown sugar
¼ teaspoon salt
1 tablespoon cornstarch
1 cup fresh orange juice
½ teaspoon grated orange rind
¼ cup butter
¼ cup raisins
3 tablespoons sherry
2 tablespoons chopped walnuts

Place sweet potatoes in 1½ quart covered casserole. In a medium saucepan, combine sugar, salt, cornstarch and orange juice. Bring to a boil, stirring constantly. Add orange rind, butter, raisins, sherry and walnuts. Pour sauce over potatoes. Cover and bake at 350° for 30 minutes.

RIP'S COOKOUT POTATOES

Rip Sewell

Serves 8

12-15 small red potatoes
½ cup butter, melted
1 clove garlic, minced
1 tablespoon Lawry's Seasoning
1 large can evaporated milk
Salt and pepper to taste

Boil potatoes with skins on for 15 minutes or until they are not quite cooked. Drain and cool. Peel and cut into ¾-inch cubes.

In a large frying pan, combine butter, garlic, Lawry's Seasoning and cubed potatoes. Cook over medium heat, adding evaporated milk, one half can at a time. Simmer about 10 minutes until the consistency of velvet. Salt and pepper to taste.

Serve with chicken or trout.

MUCH MORE THAN MUSHROOMS

Mary Barton

Serves 8-10

1 pound fresh mushrooms, sliced
4 tablespoons butter
1 cup chopped green onions
1 cup chopped celery

1 cup chopped green pepper
2 tablespoon chopped parsley
¾ cup mayonnaise
8 slices white bread, buttered
3 eggs
2 cups milk
1 can cream of mushroom soup
1 teaspoon salt
½ teaspoon pepper
1 teaspoon Worcestershire sauce
¼ teaspoon Tabasco
½ cup grated Parmesan cheese

Sauté mushrooms in butter 5 minutes. Add onions, celery, green pepper and parsley and sauté 3 minutes more. Remove from heat and stir in mayonnaise.

Remove crusts from bread, and cut into 1-inch squares. Put half the bread in buttered 3 quart casserole. Spoon mushroom mixture over bread. Cover with remaining bread.

Beat together eggs and milk. Add soup, salt, pepper, Worcestershire sauce and Tabasco. Pour over bread layer. Refrigerate 2-3 hours or overnight.

Return mixture to room temperature. Bake, uncovered, at 325° for 50 minutes. Sprinkle with Parmesan cheese and bake an additional 10 minutes or until golden brown.

Excellent companion to roast beef.

GREEN CHILE ZUCCHINI CASSEROLE

Evan Stelma

Serves 10-12

4 large yellow crookneck squash,
  halved and sliced
3 medium zucchini, halved and sliced

1 medium onion, chopped
3 tablespoons butter
1½ cups shredded Tillamook or
  cheddar cheese
1½ cups shredded Jack cheese
1 egg, lightly beaten
1 cup sour cream
2 tablespoons flour
½-1 (7 ounce) can chopped chiles
Salt and freshly ground pepper to taste
Sourdough bread crumbs
1 tablespoon butter
Paprika

Parboil squash. Drain and let stand in colander about 10 minutes to drain excess water. Sauté onion in butter until soft. Mix in cheeses, egg, sour cream, flour, chiles, salt and pepper. Mix thoroughly. Fold in squash. Pour into casserole and top with sourdough bread crumbs. Dot with butter and sprinkle with paprika. Bake at 350° for 35 minutes.

SPINACH AND ARTICHOKE CASSEROLE

Betts Simon

Serves 6-8

3 (10 ounce) packages frozen chopped
  spinach
1 (8 ounce) package cream cheese
½ cup butter or margarine
Dash of Worcestershire sauce
Salt and pepper
2 (8½ counce) cans artichoke hearts
½ cup buttered bread crumbs or
  Italian seasoned bread crumbs

Cook spinach according to package directions; drain well. While still hot, mix with cream cheese, butter and Worcestershire sauce. Season with salt and pepper to taste. Place half of the spinach in 2 quart casserole, then half of artichoke hearts. Repeat with remaining halves. Cover with bread crumbs. Bake at 350° for 30 minutes.

May be prepared early in the day and refrigerated or frozen.

Spinach Crêpes

Peter Weiss
Peter's Restaurant

1 tablespoon minced shallots
1 clove garlic, minced
4 mushrooms, chopped
Butter
2 tablespoons flour
1½ cups blanched chopped spinach

1 cup cream
¼ cup shredded Swiss cheese
2 tablespoons Parmesan cheese
Salt, pepper and thyme to taste
Crêpes, 8-inch

WHITE WINE SAUCE
2 tablespoons butter
3 tablespoons flour
1 cup half & half
1 cup chicken stock
3 tablespoons white wine
Salt, pepper and nutmeg to taste
1 tablespoon grated Parmesan cheese

Sauté shallots, garlic and mushrooms in butter. Stir in flour. Cook 2 minutes. Stir in spinach and cook until spinach loses its moisture. Stir in cream, cheeses and spices. Fill 8-inch crêpes with spinach filling and cover with WHITE WINE SAUCE.

WHITE WINE SAUCE   Melt butter and stir in flour. Cook 2 minutes, stirring. Add liquids and stir until sauce boils. Boil 1 minute and add seasonings and Parmesan cheese.

SOUTHERN CHEESE GRITS

Janet Brown

Serves 8

1 cup quick qrits
4 cups boiling water
½ teaspoon salt
½ cup butter
16 ounces jalapeno or garlic cheese
2 tablespoons Worcestershire sauce

Stir grits slowly into boiling salted water in heavy saucepan. Return to boil, reduce heat and simmer for 2½-5 minutes, stirring occasionally. Cut up butter and cheese and add to grits, continuing to stir occasionally. Add Worcestershire sauce.

May be transferred to a casserole dish for reheating and serving.

CURRIED FRUIT

Mert Grubb

Serves 10-12

⅓ cup butter, melted
¾ cup brown sugar
4 teaspoons curry powder
1 large can pear halves
1 large can apricots
1 large can peaches
1 large can pineapple chunks
10 marashino cherries, halved
Toasted almonds

Combine melted butter, sugar and curry powder. Drain fruit until dry. Place in ovenproof 2 quart casserole. Pour butter mixture over fruit. Cover with toasted almonds. Bake at 325° for 1 hour. This dish may be prepared days ahead, refrigerated and reheated until hot and bubbly.

Serve with ham, turkey or lamb.

RICE, PASTA
AND
EGG DISHES

—

WEDDING PILAF

Suzanne Manookian

Serves 4-6

1 cup long grain white rice
2 teaspoons salt, divided
2½ cups water
½ cup melted unsalted butter
  or CLARIFIED BUTTER
⅔ cup whole blanched almonds
⅔ cup dark seedless raisins
⅔ cup halved & pitted dates
Mint or parsley sprigs

Bring water and 1 teaspoon salt to a boil in a large saucepan. Add rice and boil again. Reduce heat to low and simmer until rice is tender and still firm. Drain. Add remaining salt and half the butter. Mix gently. Cover and keep warm. Heat a large skillet. Pour in remaining butter, add almonds and sauté until golden brown. Add raisins and dates and stir until thoroughly heated. Heat an ovenproof platter large enough to spread rice in a layer 1½-inches thick. Spoon rice onto platter and top with skillet contents. Garnish with mint or parsley sprigs. Serve immediately.

CLARIFIED BUTTER   Put desired amount of lightly salted butter in saucepan, filling only half full. Butter will expand. Boil over low flame about 20 minutes without stirring. Cool 10 minutes. Skim off foam. Pour clear liquid into a jar and refrigerate.

The sweet flavor of clarified butter is far superior to unsalted butter. This cooking process removes the salt and whey solids.

꧁ⴹ◎⡐꧂

COUSCOUS

Michel Lalanne

Serves 6

1 pound couscous
Chicken stock
2 hot Italian sausages, sliced
1 lamb chop, cubed

1 (3-4 pound) frying chicken,
  cut into serving pieces
1 large onion, chopped
1 red bell pepper, cut into strips
1 tablespoon cumin
4 carrots, cut into ¼-inch rounds, steamed
1 (15 ounce) can garbanzo beans, drained
¾ cup raisins
1 cup shelled, salted roasted peanuts
Salt and pepper to taste

Prepare couscous according to directions, substituting chicken stock for water. Sauté sausage pieces until cooked and browned. Remove and set aside. Add lamb cubes to same pan, brown and cook. Remove and set aside. Add chicken pieces. Sauté until cooked and browned. Remove chicken and set aside. Add onion and bell pepper and cook until lightly browned. Add cumin. Return all meats to pan. Add carrots, raisins and peanuts. Heat thoroughly. Season with salt and pepper. Toss with couscous. Keep warm on a heated platter in oven at 200° until ready to serve.

CHILE CHEESE RICE

Julie Holmquist

Serves 6-8

3 cups cooked rice
3 cups sour cream
2 (4 ounce) cans diced green chiles
¾ pound Monterey Jack cheese, shredded
½ cup shredded cheddar cheese

Lightly grease a 1½ quart casserole. Combine rice, sour cream, chiles and Jack cheese. Spoon into prepared casserole. Bake at 350° for 30 minutes. Sprinkle with cheddar. Bake 5 minutes longer or until cheese is bubbly.

Recipe is best if made ahead and baked just before serving. Very good and really easy.

❧❧❧

KIDNEY BEANS OVER RICE

Thomas R. Warde

Serves 6-8

2 large onions, thinly sliced
½ cup vegetable oil
4 (15 ounce) cans dark kidney beans, drained
2 (28 ounce) cans whole tomatoes, drained & crushed
2 bay leaves
Salt and freshly ground pepper
Freshly grated Parmesan cheese

In a stock pot or large saucepan, sauté onions in oil until transparent. Add beans, tomatoes and bay leaves. Season with salt and pepper. Sprinkle with a generous amount of Parmesan cheese. Bring to boil. Reduce heat and simmer for 2-3 hours. Sprinkle with Parmesan cheese when serving.

Serve with hamburgers or add browned ground meat and serve over cooked rice.

❧❧❧

NOODLE CASSEROLE

Carol Dumke

Serves 12

12 ounces noodles, cooked, drained
3 pounds cottage cheese
2 cups sour cream
¾ cup melted butter
⅔ cup chicken broth
2 packages dry onion soup mix

Mix together all ingredients. Spoon into a lightly greased 2½-3 quart casserole. Bake at 325° for 35 minutes.

Chicken or ham may be added for a main dish. Easy and great for large gatherings and picnics.

BARBI'S PASTA WITH SCALLOPS AND PARSLEY SAUCE

Betty Dondero

Serves 4-6

¾ pound scallops, cut horizontally
    into ¼-inch slices
1 cup half & half
½ cup heavy cream
1 cup freshly grated Parmesan cheese
⅓ cup minced parsley
Freshly grated nutmeg
Salt and freshly ground pepper

PASTA
1½ pounds fettuccini
7 quarts water
2 tablespoons salt
1 tablespoon olive oil
2 tablespoons softened unsalted butter
Minced parsley
Fresh grated Parmesan cheese

SAUCE
¼ cup fresh minced parsley
1 shallot, minced
¼ cup butter
½ cup dry white wine

SAUCE In a stainless steel or enameled skillet, sauté the parsley and shallot in butter over medium heat, about 5 minutes or until shallot softens. Add the wine and reduce over high heat, stirring constantly, until mixture has reduced to about 6 tablespoons. Add the scallops and sauté over medium heat 1 minute more. Add half & half and cream and simmer 2 minutes. Remove from heat. Stir in Parmesan, parsley and nutmeg. Season with salt and pepper. Keep sauce warm.

PASTA Bring water to a boil. Add salt and oil. Cook until *al dente*. Drain, transfer pasta to a heated platter. Toss with butter. Spoon sauce over pasta and sprinkle with parsley and Parmesan. Serve warm.

❧

RIGATONI AND BROCCOLI

Felisa Vanoff

Serves 4

1 pound fresh broccoli, cut into florets
¼ cup butter
⅓ cup olive oil
3 cloves garlic, minced
Red pepper flakes (optional)
1 pound rigatoni
Salt and freshly ground pepper
Parmesan cheese, grated

Steam broccoli in enough salted water to just cover them. Do not overcook. In a large skillet, melt butter and oil. Sauté garlic until transparent, being careful not to burn, and add red pepper flakes, if desired. Add drained broccoli, toss and set aside. Cook the rigatoni in boiling salted water, or reserved water from cooked broccoli may also be used. Drain the rigatoni and add to the broccoli mixture. Stir gently to mix carefully. Season with salt and pepper. Top with Parmesan cheese and serve immediately.

OYSTERS TETRAZZINI

Barbara Dutcher

Serves 8

1½ quarts fresh oysters,
    liquid drained and reserved
Salt and freshly ground pepper
Tabasco
1 pound sliced bacon
4 cups medium-thin cream sauce
2 tablespoons prepared mustard
8 ounces spaghetti, cooked, drained
1½ cups shredded Cheddar cheese
Parsley
Paprika

Sprinkle drained oysters with salt and pepper. Dash each oyster with Tabasco. Wrap each oyster in a slice of bacon. Secure with a toothpick. Place on a broiler pan. Bake at 325° until bacon is crisp, being careful not to overcook. Meanwhile, make the cream sauce. Add mustard to ½ cup reserved oyster liquid. Season with salt and pepper. Set aside. When oysters are cooked, remove from oven. Turn oven up to 350°. Remove toothpicks from oysters.

Butter a 4 quart casserole. Place a layer of cooked spaghetti on bottom. Top with a layer of oysters. Spoon a layer of cream sauce over oysters. Sprinkle with a layer of cheese. Repeat using all ingredients. Top with parsley and sprinkle with paprika. Bake at 350° for 30-40 minutes or until cheese has melted and nicely browned.

Serve with a green salad and French bread.

❧❦❧

LOUIE'S FETTUCCINI IN GARLIC SAUCE

Louie Mallane
Louie's Pizza and Italian Restaurant

Serves 2-4

½ pound egg or spinach fettuccini
½ cup chopped mushrooms
½ cup chopped green onions
1 clove garlic, finely chopped
1 tablespoon fresh chopped basil
4 tablespoons butter
¼ cup olive oil
Salt and freshly ground pepper
½ cup freshly grated Parmesan cheese

Cook the noodles in boiling salted water until *al dente*, 10-12 minutes. Drain well. Sauté the mushrooms, green onions, garlic and basil in the butter and olive oil over medium-high heat for about 3 minutes. Remove from heat. Add the drained noodles. Season with salt and pepper and sprinkle generously with Parmesan cheese. Mix well and serve immediately on warmed plates.

If you are going to use Parmesan cheese, there is only one way to go—fresh! Buy it in the block, and grate it only when you are going to use it.

GREEK ZUCCHINI AND MACARONI

Marilyn Stavros

Serves 4

3 cups zucchini, cut into 1-inch slices
½ cup chopped onion

¼ cup oil
2-3 medium tomatoes, chopped
   or 1 (16 ounce) can whole tomatoes
¾ teaspoon dried basil
   or 1½ teaspoons dried mint
1½ teaspoons dried dill
¾ teaspoon salt (omit if using
   canned tomatoes)
⅛ teaspoon pepper
½ cup plain yogurt
1 cup uncooked macaroni

In a large skillet, sauté zucchini and onion in the oil until tender, about 5 minutes. Add the tomatoes, basil or mint, dill, salt and pepper. Simmer 15 minutes. Stir in yogurt and blend until heated through, about 2-3 minutes. Cook macaroni in boiling salted water, drain. Serve zucchini over hot macaroni.

This is a quick, easy and inexpensive recipe for gardeners, and a healthy one for all!

❧🕉🕉❧

LINGUINE WITH CLAM SAUCE

Jean Ray

Serves 4

6 pounds fresh clams,
   or 2 (6½ ounce) cans chopped clams
2 cups cold water
¼ cup dry white wine
1 small onion, diced
1 bay leaf
1½ teaspoons minced garlic
6 tablespoons butter
3 tablespoons minced parsley
⅓ cup dry white wine
Salt and pepper
1 pound linguine

For fresh clams, rinse clams with cold running water to remove sand. Place in a pot large enough to hold them comfortably. Add water, wine, onion and bay leaf. Cover. Bring to a boil on high heat, and steam for 7-10 minutes until shells open. Discard any clams which do not open. Drain. Reserving liquid remove clams from shells. For canned clams, drain and reserve liquid.

Sauté garlic in butter in a large skillet over medium heat being careful not to burn garlic. Add clams, clam liquid and parsley. Stir until well blended and reduce by simmering, about 4 minutes. Add wine and reduce 2 minutes more. Season with salt and pepper. Cook linguine 3-5 minutes for fresh pasta, and 5-7 minutes for packaged. Add linguine to clam mixture, toss and heat. Serve hot.

SPRINGTIME PASTA

Roxanne M. Sanderson

Serves 4-6 as main course
6-8 as first course

½ cup unsalted butter
1 medium onion, minced
1 large clove garlic, minced
1 pound thin asparagus,
   cut diagonally into 1-inch slices
½ pound mushrooms, thinly sliced
6 ounces cauliflower, broken into florets
1 medium zucchini, cut into ¼-inch slices
1 small carrot cut into
   ⅛-inch diagonal slices
1 cup fresh young peas
Juice from ½ lemon
1 cup heavy cream
½ cup chicken stock
1 tablespoon fresh basil, chopped
   or 2 teaspoons dried basil
2 ounces prosciutto, chopped
5 green onions, chopped
Salt and freshly ground pepper
1 pound fettuccine or linguine,
   cooked *al dente*
½ cup freshly grated Parmesan

Heat a wok or large, deep skillet over medium heat. Add butter, onion and garlic. Sauté until softened, about 2 minutes. Mix in asparagus, mushrooms, cauliflower, zucchini, carrot and peas. Sprinkle with lemon juice. Stir fry for 2 minutes. Increase heat to high. Add cream, stock and basil. Boil until liquid is slightly reduced, about 3 minutes. Stir in prosciutto and green onion. Cook 1 minute more. Season to taste with salt and pepper. Add pasta and cheese, tossing until thoroughly combined and pasta is heated through.

❧⊘❧

LAZY ITALIAN LASAGNE

Donna Frans

Serves 8

1 package lasagne noodles
1 pound hamburger
2 cloves garlic, minced
1 tablespoon Italian seasoning
1 medium onion, chopped
Salt and pepper to taste
1 large jar spaghetti sauce
   (Ragu Homestyle)
2 medium zucchini, thinly sliced
12 large mushrooms, sliced
1 pint cottage cheese or ricotta cheese
2 cups shredded Mozzarella cheese

Cook noodles in boiling water until three-quarters done. Drain and rinse in cold water. Cook hamburger in skillet with garlic, Italian seasoning, onion, salt and pepper until done. Drain excess fat. Add spaghetti sauce. Simmer for 15 minutes.

In a large baking dish, layer alternately noodles, zucchini, mushrooms, cottage or ricotta cheese, spaghetti sauce and Mozzarella cheese. Top with lots of Mozzarella cheese. Bake at 350° for 45 minutes.

EGG ROLL CANNELLONI

Peggy Dean

Serves 6

6 ounces mild Italian sausage
10 ounces frozen chopped spinach, thawed

1 pound ricotta cheese
2 egg yolks
1 cup grated Parmesan cheese
⅛ teaspoon pepper
¾ teaspoon crushed fennel seed
¾ teaspoon oregano leaves
12 egg rolls
1 (15½ ounce) can marinara sauce
  (Golden Grain)
1 pound sliced Teleme or Jack cheese

Remove casings from sausages. Break up meat in an 8 to 10-inch frying pan. Stir over medium heat until browned and crumbly. Drain off fat. Squeeze liquid from spinach. Mix sausage, spinach, ricotta cheese, egg yolks, Parmesan cheese and spices. Mound ⅓ cup filling along one long edge of each egg roll. Roll to enclose. Spread half of marinara sauce in a shallow baking dish about 9x13-inches. Place cannelloni, seam side down, slightly apart in sauce. Spread with remaining sauce. Top each cannelloni with a slice of Teleme. Bake, uncovered, at 400° for 30-40 minutes. Let stand 10 minutes before serving.

❧❧❧

CREAMED EGGS AND MUSHROOMS

Mrs. R.B. Neely

Serves 6

12 hard boiled eggs
1 clove garlic, minced
1 cup butter, divided

1 teaspoon salt
½ teaspoon freshly ground pepper
1 green pepper, seeded
1 (6 ounce) can sliced mushrooms,
  undrained
1 can beef consomme
1 cup cream
2 tablespoons flour
1 tablespoon dry mustard
½ cup sherry
1 teaspoon Worcestershire sauce
Paprika

While still warm, halve the eggs lengthwise. Mash the yolks with garlic and half of the butter. Season with ½ teaspoon salt and ¼ teaspoon pepper. Stuff egg whites with this mixture. Place in a lightly greased baking dish, just large enough to hold eggs comfortably. Blanch green pepper until tender and drain. Cut into strips.

Combine mushroom liquid, consomme and cream. Set aside. In the top of a double boiler, combine the rest of the butter, flour, mustard, sherry and Worcestershire sauce. Season with remaining salt and pepper. Add consomme mixture. Cook over simmering water until thickened. Fold in mushrooms and green peppers. Pour over eggs. Serve warm.

GREEN CHILE PIE

George F. Weston, Jr.

Serves 6-8

1-2 large cans whole green chiles, seeded, cut into strips
2 cups shredded Mozzarella cheese
2 cups shredded Monterey Jack cheese
4 eggs

Lightly grease an 8 or 9-inch ovenproof pie plate. Line bottom of plate by overlapping chiles. Mix shredded cheeses together and pile pyramid style in middle of plate. Beat eggs together and pour over cheese. Do not mix. Bake at 325° for 40-50 minutes or until golden.

Keep out of sight or it will be devoured immediately. Serve while it's hot, and it's yummmmmmmmy!

BRUNCH CASSEROLE

Penny Paynter

Serves 6

5 slices thick sourdough bread
3 cups shredded cheddar cheese
1½ pounds link sausage, cooked, drained and crumbled
5 eggs
2¼ cups milk
¾ teaspoon dry mustard
1 can cream of mushroom soup
⅔ cup milk

Lightly grease a 9x13-inch baking dish. Break bread slices into 2-inch pieces. Line bottom of baking dish. Top with cheese, then sausage. In a small bowl, beat eggs, milk and mustard. Pour over sausage. Cover and refrigerate overnight.

Remove from refrigerator. Mix soup and milk and pour evenly over casserole. Bake, uncovered, at 300° for 1 hour. Serve hot.

CHEESE SOUFFLÉ

Ricard Ohrstrom

Serves 6-8

3 tablespoons butter
4 tablespoons flour
1½ cups milk
6 egg yolks, beaten
1 cup shredded sharp cheddar cheese
1 cup shredded Swiss cheese
1 teaspoon dry mustard
Cayenne pepper
⅛ teaspoon nutmeg
8 egg whites
¼ teaspoon cream of tartar

Make a wax paper collar to extend a 2 quart soufflé dish. Melt butter, add flour and stir. Slowly add milk and cook until thick. Add in beaten egg yolks very slowly, stirring constantly. Add cheeses, mustard, cayenne pepper to taste, and nutmeg. Mix well and set aside. Beat egg whites until foamy. Add cream of tartar and beat until stiff. Fold into cheese mixture. Pour mixture into prepared soufflé dish and bake at 375° for 40-50 minutes.

SOUFFLÉED GREEN CHILE ENCHILADA

Sue Bridgman

Serves 4

7-8 corn tortillas
Salad oil
1 (7 ounce) can green chile salsa
4 eggs, separated
1 tablespoon flour
1¾ cups shredded Monterey Jack cheese
3-4 canned California green chiles
1 mild red pepper, sliced

Fry tortillas in oil and dip in salsa. Put one tortilla in bottom of 7 or 8-inch ungreased casserole which is at least 2 inches deep. Arrange the remaining tortillas, overlapping, around the sides and slightly over the bottom center tortilla. Beat egg whites until stiff. Set aside. With same beater, whip egg yolks until slightly thickened, then beat in flour. Stir in 1 cup of cheese. Rinse chiles, remove seeds and pith, then chop. Add chopped chiles to egg yolks, and then a little of the egg white. Fold yolk mixture into remaining whites and pour into tortilla-lined dish. Fold tortillas down over filling. Spoon remaining salsa onto tortillas, then sprinkle evenly with remaining cheese. Bake, uncovered, at 375° for 30 minutes or until center is set. Garnish with red pepper and serve.

THREE-CHEESE EGGS

Burnice Dolac

Serves 4

3-4 shallots, minced
4 tablespoons butter
1 can cheddar cheese soup
1 cup half & half
⅛ teaspoon Worcestershire sauce or bitters
Salt and freshly ground pepper
6 slices Swiss cheese,
    or enough to cover bottom of pan
4 eggs
2 tablespoons sherry
Parmesan cheese, grated

In a saucepan sauté shallots in butter over low heat until tender. Add soup and half & half. Stir until smooth. Add either Worcestershire sauce or bitters and season with salt and pepper. Remove from heat.

Line the bottom and sides of a buttered 8-inch square dish with cheese slices. Break 4 eggs carefully over cheese slices. Add sherry to sauce. Pour sauce carefully over eggs. Sprinkle with Parmesan cheese. Bake at 350° for 10-12 minutes or until eggs are cooked and sauce is bubbly. Watch carefully. Serve immediately.

Great for Sunday brunch or supper.

BREADS

MORMON HERB BREAD

Helen Wooley Willis

Makes 1 loaf

2 yeast cakes dissolved in
 ¼ cup warm water (110°)

¾ cup scalded milk, cooled to lukewarm
1½ tablespoons sugar
1 tablespoon salt
4 tablespoons butter, softened
1 egg, slightly beaten
1 tablespoon celery seed
1 tablespoon nutmeg
1 tablespoon sage
1 tablespoon caraway seed
4 cups flour

Mix together all ingredients except flour. Add flour gradually, mixing well. Let rise to double in bulk. Knead down and shape into round loaf. Let rise to double in bulk and bake at 350° for 45-60 minutes.

Delicious with Durkee Sauce and Corned Beef.

SEMMEL KNÖDEL GERMAN DUMPLINGS

Mary Longley

10 rolls (day-old, but not rock hard)
1¾ cup milk, lukewarm
1 tablespoon butter
1 small onion, minced
1 egg, beaten
Salt to taste
⅓ cup chopped parsley
Flour for dusting

Cut rolls into small cubes. Place in a large bowl and cover with milk. Let soak.

Sauté onion in butter. Add to bread cube mixture. Add egg, salt and parsley and knead mixture together to make a dough. If very sticky, add a few more bread crumbs. Form dough into 2½ to 3½-inch diameter balls. Dust with small amount of flour.

Bring a large pot of salted water to a simmering, not rolling boil. With spoon, lower balls into water. Cook 15-20 minutes.

Serve with gravy, goulash, or bouillon soup.

Danish Filled Coffee Cake

Ann Boughton

Serves 6-8

CAKE
2 cups flour, sifted
¾ cup brown sugar
¼ cup sugar

½ teaspoon salt
½ teaspoon baking soda
½ teaspoon nutmeg
1 egg, beaten
1 cup buttermilk
½ cup vegetable oil

FILLING
½ cup brown sugar
3 teaspoons cinnamon
2 tablespoons flour
2 tablespoons butter, melted
1 cup chopped walnuts

CAKE   Sift together all dry ingredients for cake. Add egg, buttermilk and vegetable oil. Mix well.

FILLING   In a separate bowl combine ingredients for filling and mix well. Pour half of cake batter into greased 9x9-inch pan. Sprinkle with half filling mixture. Repeat procedure with other half cake batter and filling mix. Bake at 350° for 30-40 minutes.

A favorite Christmas morning coffee cake for children.

❦

Quick Blueberry Coffee Cake

Betty Fisher

Serves 20

½ cup butter
1 cup sugar

3 eggs
1 cup sour cream
2 cups flour
1 teaspoon baking soda
½ teaspoon salt
1 teaspoon vanilla
2 cups fresh or frozen blueberries
½ cup brown sugar
½ cup chopped pecans
½ teaspoon cinnamon
2 tablespoons powdered sugar (optional)

Mix butter and sugar until light in food processor using metal blade. Add eggs and sour cream and blend a few seconds, then add flour, baking soda, salt and vanilla and blend until smooth. Carefully fold in blueberries. Pour half of cake batter in bottom of a 9 x 13-inch greased baking dish. Mix together brown sugar, pecans and cinnamon, and spread evenly over batter. Pour remaining batter over top and bake at 350° for 45 minutes or until cake tests done. If desired, top with powdered sugar. Cool before cutting.

BANANA BREAD

Jeanne Lane

Makes 1 loaf

½ cup butter or shortening
1 cup sugar
2 eggs
¼ teaspoon salt
3 ripe bananas, mashed
½ cup chopped nuts
1 teaspoon baking soda mixed in
    1 teaspoon water
1½ cups flour, sifted

Cream butter and sugar. Beat in 2 whole eggs and salt. Add mashed bananas and chopped nuts. Stir in baking soda. Add flour and beat well. Pour into greased 9x5-inch loaf pan and bake at 350° for 1 hour.

BUTTERSCOTCH BANANA BREAD

Gayle Stevenson

Makes 1 loaf

1½ cups mashed ripe bananas
   (about 3 medium)
½ cup sugar
¼ cup brown sugar

2 eggs
4 tablespoons melted butter
1 teaspoon vanilla
1 cup bran
1½ cups whole wheat flour
2 teaspoons baking powder
½ teaspoon baking soda
½ teaspoon cinnamon
½ teaspoon nutmeg
½ teaspoon salt
¼ cup milk
1⅓ cup chopped pecans
1 (6 ounce) package
   butterscotch morsels

In a large bowl combine bananas, sugars, eggs, butter and vanilla. Mix well. Mix in bran and let sit for 5 minutes. Sift together flour, baking powder, baking soda, cinnamon, nutmeg and salt. Combine with banana mixture. Gradually add milk. Mix well. Stir in 1 cup pecans and butterscotch morsels. Pour into a greased 9x5x3-inch loaf pan. Sprinkle top with remaining ⅓ cup pecans. Bake at 350° for 60-70 minutes. Cool 30 minutes and remove from pan.

ZUCCHINI BREAD

Jeanie Kearney

Makes 2 large loaves

3 cups flour
½ teaspoon baking powder
1 teaspoon baking soda
1 teaspoon salt
3 teaspoons cinnamon
3 eggs
2 cups sugar or 1¾ cups honey
1 cup oil
2 teaspoons vanilla
2-3 cups shredded zucchini
¾ cup chopped nuts

Combine flour, baking powder, baking soda, salt and cinnamon. In a separate bowl, beat eggs until foamy. Add sugar, oil, vanilla and zucchini; beat well. Add dry ingredients and nuts. Stir well. Pour into 2 greased and floured 9x5-inch pans. Bake at 325° for 1 hour.

MOM'S APPLESAUCE BREAD

Lynn Campion

Makes 2 small loaves

1 cup sugar
½ cup butter, softened
1 egg
1½ cups applesauce
2 cups flour
1 teaspoon vanilla
1 teaspoon salt
2 teaspoons baking soda
½ teaspoon cinnamon

Cream butter and sugar together. Add egg and mix well. Add remaining ingredients and mix just until blended. Pour into 2 (7⅜x3⅝-inch) greased and floured bread pans. Bake at 350° for 1 hour.

CARROT RAISIN NUT BREAD

Starr Weekes
Starr's Stuff

Makes 1 loaf

1½ cups raisins
1 cup sugar or ½ cup honey

¾ cup all-purpose flour
¾ cup whole wheat flour
½ teaspoon salt
½ teaspoon cinnamon
½ teaspoon baking soda
⅛ teaspoon baking powder
1 egg
½ cup oil (must be oil)
1 teaspoon vanilla
1 cup shredded carrots
1 cup chopped walnuts

Soak raisins in hot water for a few minutes. Drain. Mix thoroughly all ingredients until well blended. Pour into greased and floured 9x5-inch loaf pan. Bake at 350° for 1 hour or until done.

Variation   *Substitute 1 cup shredded zucchini for 1 cup carrots.*

YUM YUM BREAD

Pam Wells

Makes 1 loaf

¾ cup unbleached flour, sifted
¼ cup cracked wheat
2 cups whole wheat flour
¾ teaspoon salt
1½ teaspoons baking soda
2 cups buttermilk
½ cup brown sugar, loosely packed

Mix ingredients together. Place in a greased and floured 9x5-inch loaf pan. Bake at 350° for 1 hour or until it springs back to the touch.

GINGER CORNMEAL MUFFINS

Donna Kelsey

Makes 16 muffins

1 cup cornmeal
1 cup flour
2 teaspoons sugar
1 teaspoon salt
3 teaspoons baking powder
½ cup chopped, crystallized ginger
2 large eggs, beaten
1 cup milk
4 tablespoons melted butter

Stir into a bowl the cornmeal, flour, sugar, salt and baking powder. Mix in the crystallized ginger. Add the beaten eggs and milk and blend well. Gently mix in the melted butter. Brush muffin pans with melted butter. Spoon in batter until ¾ full. Bake at 425° for 15-20 minutes until browned and baked through. Check after 10 minutes of baking, and if browning too fast, turn heat down to 400°.

MUMMIE'S BRAN MUFFINS

Carol Dumke

Makes 5½ dozen

5 cups all purpose flour
   or 2½ cups all purpose flour and
   2½ cups whole wheat flour

1 teaspoon salt
4 cups All-Bran cereal
2 cups 40% Bran Flakes cereal
2 cups chopped dates
1 cup chopped nuts, or to taste
1 cup golden raisins
2 cups boiling water
5 teaspoons baking soda
2 cups brown sugar
1 cup shortening
4 eggs
1 quart buttermilk

Sift together flour and salt. Combine flour mixture, All-Bran, Bran Flakes, dates, nuts and raisins. Set aside.

Mix boiling water and baking soda. Set aside to cool.

In a large bowl cream sugar and shortening. Stir in eggs one at a time. Beat well. Stir in buttermilk and water mixture. Stir in bran mixture. Cover tightly and refrigerate 12 hours or more. Do not stir again.

Drop batter by tablespoonsful into greased muffin tins. Bake at 375° for 20 minutes.

Batter keeps for up to 6 weeks in refrigerator. Make muffins fresh as needed in the morning.

BOSTON BLUEBERRY MUFFINS

Maribeth Dashe

Makes 1 dozen

1 cup all purpose flour
1 cup whole wheat flour
½ cup sugar
1 tablespoon baking powder
½ teaspoon salt
½ teaspoon cinnamon
1½-2 cups fresh or frozen (unthawed) blueberries
½ cup butter, melted
½ cup milk
2 eggs
½ teaspoon vanilla
1½ tablespoons sugar, for topping

In a large bowl combine flours, sugar, baking powder, salt and cinnamon. In a separate bowl, toss 1 tablespoon of the dry ingredients with the berries and set aside.

Cool butter slightly and stir in milk, eggs and vanilla. Mix well. Add egg mixture to dry ingredients and stir until well-moistened. Stir in berries.

Spoon batter into well-buttered muffin pans or cups. Sprinkle muffin tops with reserved 1½ tablespoons sugar. Bake at 425° for 15 minutes or until golden brown. Let muffins stand 5 minutes before removing from pans.

If using larger quantities of blueberries, let muffins cool completely before removing from pans. Reheat at 350° for 7 minutes before serving.

REALLY LIGHT BUTTERMILK PANCAKES

Alan Stevenson

Serves 4

1¾ cups buttermilk
1 cup plus 1 tablespoon flour
1 teaspoon baking soda
1 teaspoon baking powder
¼ teaspoon sugar
1 tablespoon melted butter
3 eggs, separated

Combine buttermilk, flour, baking soda, baking powder, sugar, melted butter and egg yolks. Mix well. In a separate bowl, beat egg whites until stiff and fold into buttermilk mixture. Cook on hot griddle.

SOURDOUGH HOT CAKES

Kevin Swigert
U.S. Nordic Ski Team
4 Time Winner
NBC *Survival of the Fittest*

SOURDOUGH STARTER
3 potatoes, peeled

3 cups flour
1 package yeast
¼ cup water

HOT CAKE BATTER
2 cups STARTER
¼ cup sugar
Salt to taste
¼ cup vegetable oil
1 egg
1 teaspoon baking soda
Milk

STARTER Cut potatoes into small pieces and boil until soft. Pour off and save water. Combine flour and enough potato water to make slightly thicker than pancake batter. Combine yeast with ¼ cup lukewarm water; dissolve and mix into batter. Place batter in a large enough bowl to fill only one-third full, cover loosely, and allow to stand at room temperature for 2 days. Replace amount used with equal amounts of flour and water, let work, then place in refrigerator if not to be used soon.

BATTER Place 2 cups of STARTER in a bowl. Mix in sugar, salt, oil, egg and stir until well mixed. Add baking soda and stir well. If too thick, add enough milk to make a runny batter. Pour by spoonfuls onto a medium-hot greased griddle. If the taste is slightly bitter, add more soda, or if they do not brown, add more sugar.

Serve with Chokecherry syrup.

RICOTTA CHEESE PANCAKES

Pat Feldman

Serves 4-6

1 teaspoon baking powder
½ pound ricotta cheese
⅔ cup milk
½ cup flour
3 eggs, separated
⅛ teaspoon salt
Oil for frying

In a large mixing bowl, beat baking powder, cheese, milk, flour and egg yolks. In separate bowl, beat egg whites with salt until soft peaks form. Fold into cheese mixture.

Lightly coat a moderately hot griddle with oil. Drop pancakes by tablespoonsful. Turn once when edges brown. Pancakes will be slightly moist and taste like custard.

GIANT OVEN PANCAKE

Sandy and Dale Elmer

Serves 4

3 tablespoons butter
3 eggs
½ cup flour
¼ teaspoon salt
½ cup milk
Powdered sugar
Maple flavored syrup or lemon wedges

Melt butter in a 10-inch ovenproof skillet over low heat. In a mixing bowl beat eggs until well mixed. Add flour and salt; beat until nearly smooth. Stir in milk and melted butter with a spoon until smooth. Pour batter into warm skillet. Bake 15 minutes at 450°, then lower oven to 350° and bake 10-15 minutes longer. Remove from oven. Spoon a little powdered sugar into a strainer and sift over the finished pancake. Cut into 4 pieces and serve with maple syrup or lemon wedges.

SKIER'S FRENCH TOAST

Peggy Fuller

Serves 6-8

2 tablespoons corn syrup (light or dark)
½ cup butter
1 cup brown sugar
1 loaf unsliced white bread, crust trimmed
5 eggs
1½ cups milk
1 teaspoon vanilla
¼ teaspoon salt

In a small saucepan, mix syrup, butter and sugar. Simmer over medium heat until syrupy. Pour over bottom of 9x13-inch pan. Slice bread into 12-16 slices. Place over syrup mixture.

Beat together eggs, milk, vanilla and salt. Pour over bread. Cover and refrigerate overnight.

Bake, uncovered, at 350° for 45 minutes. Serve hot or warm. Can be reheated.

DESSERTS

CHOCOLATE ORANGE TORTE

Bernice Ludwig

Serves 10

1 cup chocolate wafers, crushed
¼ cup melted butter
1½ tablespoons sugar
3 ounces semi-sweet chocolate
1 ounce unsweetened chocolate
3 tablespoons water
5 eggs, separated
1 teaspoon grated orange peel
2 tablespoons Grand Marnier
¼ teaspoon cream of tartar
¼ cup sugar

Combine wafers, butter and sugar. Press into buttered 9-inch springform pan. Bake at 350° for 10 minutes. Cool. In top of double boiler combine chocolates and water. Stir over hot water until melted. Beat egg yolks slightly and add to chocolate, blending with a wire whisk, until smooth. Add orange peel and liqueur.

In a separate bowl beat together egg whites and cream of tartar until stiff. Beat sugar in slowly. Mix about ⅓ of egg whites into chocolate mixture with a wire whisk. Gently fold remaining egg whites into chocolate mixture. Pour into crust and freeze, uncovered, until firm, about 2 hours. Wrap torte in plastic wrap until ready to serve. Garnish with fresh orange curls or thinly sliced orange rounds cut half way through and twisted.

❦

FROZEN CHOCOLATE MOUSSE TORTE

Catherine Crosson

Serves 10

1 (7 ounce) package almond paste
1 tablespoon cocoa
5 eggs
6 ounces semi-sweet chocolate, melted
2 teaspoons instant coffee
1 tablespoon brandy or other liqueur
2 tablespoons sugar
½ cup whipping cream, whipped

In a food processor break almond paste into small pieces. Add cocoa and 2 of the eggs. Whip until mixture is smooth. Pour into greased and floured 9-inch round pan with removable bottom. Bake at 375° for 15 minutes or until cake springs back when touched lightly. Cool on rack.

Separate 2 of remaining eggs. In a large mixing bowl beat egg yolks with remaining whole egg. Beat in melted chocolate, coffee and brandy.

Beat egg whites until foamy. Gradually add sugar and beat until moist, stiff peaks form. Fold into chocolate mixture. Fold in whipped cream. Spread chocolate mousse over almond torte and freeze. Thaw 10 minutes before serving.

A very rich two-layered chocolate dessert.

HAZELNUT TORTEN

Michelle Praggastis

Serves 12

MERINGUE LAYERS
12 egg whites
⅛ teaspoon salt
2¼ cups sugar
1½ cup toasted, skinned and
    finely chopped hazelnuts

1½ cups toasted and finely chopped
    almonds
¾ cup toasted and finely chopped pecans

BUTTERCREAM FILLING
1 cup sugar
½ cup water
Few drops fresh lemon juice
1 pound unsalted butter,
    at room temperature
8 egg yolks
6 ounces semi-sweet chocolate, melted
2 tablespoons Kahlua
2 tablespoons Grand Marnier
½ cup slivered almonds

MERINGUE   Preheat oven to 325°. Beat egg whites with salt until stiff. Combine sugar and nuts and gently fold into whites. Cut parchment into 4 (4x12-inch) rectangles. Place two strips on each baking sheet and butter generously. Spread meringue evenly over parchment, and bake 20-30 minutes, or until crusty on top. Cool slightly. Cover meringue with another baking sheet, invert and gently peel off paper.

BUTTERCREAM   Combine sugar, water and lemon juice in small saucepan. Shake gently until sugar dissolves, then heat without stirring to 230° on candy thermometer. Cream butter, set aside.

Beat egg yolks until foamy. With mixer on high speed, add sugar syrup to yolks in thin stream and beat until mixture stands in soft peaks. Reduce speed to medium, and beat in butter a small amount at a time. Divide buttercream in half. Divide one portion in half again. Add melted chocolate to larger portion, and flavor smaller portions with Kahlua and Grand Marnier.

To assemble: Spread one layer of meringue with Kahlua mixture. Top with second layer of meringue, and spread with Grand Marnier mixture. Add third layer of meringue, and spread with half of chocolate mixture. Add last layer of meringue, and frost top and sides with remaining buttercream. Sprinkle with slivered almonds.

CHOCOLATE TORTE SUPREME

Eddie Dumke

Serves 12

10 (1 ounce) squares semi-sweet chocolate
1¼ cups butter
12 eggs
3 cups sifted powdered sugar, divided
1½ cups sifted flour, divided

CREAMY CHOCOLATE FROSTING
6 (1 ounce) squares unsweetened chocolate
½ cup butter, softened
6 cups sifted powdered sugar
1 cup whipping cream
2 teaspoons vanilla
¼ cup marzipan or almond paste

Grease and flour 4 (9-inch) cake pans. Combine chocolate and butter in top of a double boiler. Bring water to a boil. Reduce heat to low and cook, stirring occasionally, until chocolate melts.

Beat 6 eggs at high speed of electric mixer until thick and lemon-colored. Gradually add 1½ cups sugar, beating 5-10 minutes. Add ¾ cup flour, beating well. Continue beating and gradually add half of the chocolate mixture. Pour batter into 2 prepared pans, spreading evenly. Bake at 350° for 25 minutes or until wooden toothpick inserted in center comes out clean. While layers bake, repeat mixing procedure with remaining ingredients.

Cool all baked layers in pans 10 minutes. Remove from pans and cool layers completely. Roll marzipan to ¼-inch thickness and cut to fit size of cake. Spread CREAMY CHOCOLATE FROSTING between all layers. Place marzipan between second and third layers. Frost top and sides of cake. Store in refrigerator.

CREAMY CHOCOLATE FROSTING   Place chocolate in top of a double boiler. Bring water to a boil, reduce heat to low. Cook stirring occasionally, until chocolate melts. Cream butter; alternately add sugar, chocolate and whipping cream, beating until light and fluffy. Stir in vanilla.

POPPY SEED CAKE

Vance Carter
Copper Basin Restaurant

Serves 10-12

2½ cups yellow cake mix
½ cup vanilla pudding mix
½ cup oil
½ cup sherry
4 eggs
1 cup poppy seeds

Mix cake mix, pudding, oil, sherry, eggs and poppy seeds. Pour into greased and floured bundt pan, and bake at 350° for 55 minutes.

BLITZ TORTE CAKE

Susan Hall

Serves 6-8

½ cup sugar
⅓ cup butter
¾ teaspoon vanilla

4 eggs, separated
1 cup plus 2 tablespoons flour
1 teaspoon baking powder
½ teaspoon salt
¼ cup milk
1 cup sugar
2 cups heavy cream, whipped
4 tablespoons Cointreau or Grand Marnier
2 cups sliced strawberries

Cream together sugar, butter and vanilla. Beat egg yolks and add to creamed mixture. Mix well. Sift together flour, baking powder and salt. Add to creamed mixture alternately with milk.

Grease and flour 2 (9-inch) cake pans and spread mixture to within 1 inch of edges of pan. Beat egg whites until stiff. Gradually add 1 cup sugar. Beat until stiff. Spread meringue over cake mixture leaving about ½ inch of cake showing. Bake at 350° for 25-30 minutes. Cool and turn out.

Flavor whipped cream with Cointreau or Grand Marnier. Toss strawberries with 2 tablespoons remaining liqueur.

To assemble   Spread half of flavored whipped cream over one cake layer. Put half of strawberries on whipped cream. Top with second layer of cake. Repeat cream layer followed by strawberry layer.

Serve within 1 hour of assembly.

MARNIE'S KAHLUA CAKE

Renée Kreilkamp

Serves 10-12

1 Swiss chocolate cake mix
1 box (5⅝ ounces)
   instant chocolate pudding
⅓ cup Kahlua
⅔ cup oil
4 eggs
2 cups sour cream
8 ounces chocolate chips
1 cup chopped nuts

Combine cake mix, pudding, Kahlua, oil, eggs and sour cream. Beat until well blended. Stir in chocolate chips and nuts. Pour into lightly greased and floured bundt pan. Bake at 350° for 50-55 minutes.

Serve lightly dusted with powdered sugar with ice cream or whipped cream flavored with Kahlua.

SOUR CREAM DESSERT RING

Karen Curry

Serves 8-10

¾ cup butter
1½ cups sugar

1 cup sour cream
½ teaspoon vanilla
2 eggs
¼ teaspoon salt
1 teaspoon baking powder
2 cups flour
2 tablespoons brown sugar
1 teaspoon instant cocoa
½ teaspoon cinnamon
½ cup pecans

Cream together butter and sugar. Add sour cream, vanilla and eggs. Beat until smooth. In a separate bowl, combine salt, baking powder and flour. Fold into sour cream mixture. Mix together brown sugar, cocoa, cinnamon and pecans. Pour half of batter into a greased and floured bundt pan. Sprinkle with half of the nut mixture. Pour in remaining batter and sprinkle with the rest of the nut mixture.

Bake at 350° for 50-60 minutes. Serve with ice cream or whipped cream.

NANCY'S ONE BOWL CHOCOLATE CAKE

Louise Gallagher

Serves 10-12

1 cup brown sugar
1 cup applesauce, unsweetened
2-3 teaspoons instant coffee grains
2 cups flour
½ teaspoon cinnamon

½ teaspoon salt
1 teaspoon baking soda
3 tablespoons cocoa
1 cup safflower oil

FROSTING
⅓ cup rum
½ cup cocoa
¼ cup instant coffee grains
3-4 tablespoons cornstarch
1½ cups sugar
½ teaspoon salt
1 cup whipping cream
1 cup milk
1 teaspoon butter
2 teaspoons vanilla

Combine all cake ingredients in one, large mixing bowl. Beat well. Pour into greased and floured 10-inch springform pan or 2 (8-inch) layer cake pans. Bake at 350° for 25-30 minutes for 10-inch pan or 35 minutes for 8-inch pans or until cake tests done with a toothpick.

FROSTING   Combine all frosting ingredients in heavy saucepan. Cook over medium heat until thick. Cool. Frost cake while frosting and cake still are warm.

CHOCOLATE BANANA CAKE

Peggy Rose

Serves 10-12

2½ cups flour
2 cups sugar
1 teaspoon baking soda
1 cup butter or margarine
1¼ cup water
4 tablespoons cocoa

½ cup buttermilk
2 eggs, beaten
1 teaspoon vanilla
2 bananas, mashed

CHOCOLATE CREAM CHEESE FROSTING
1 (8 ounce) package cream cheese
1 tablespoon milk
1 teaspoon vanilla
Dash of salt
5 cups powdered sugar, sifted
3 (1 ounce) unsweetened chocolate
   squares, melted
Pecans, chopped (optional)

Mix flour, sugar and soda in bowl. Bring butter, water and cocoa to a boil in pan. Pour over dry ingredients and mix well. Add buttermilk, eggs and vanilla. Beat well. Pour into greased and floured 9x13-inch pan. Bake at 350° for 30 minutes or until done. When cool, cut in half and spread mashed bananas between layers. Frost top and sides with CHOCOLATE CREAM CHEESE FROSTING.

FROSTING   Combine cream cheese, milk, vanilla and salt. Add sugar, one cup at a time. Stir in melted chocolate. Add chopped pecans to frosting if desired.

❧❀│❀☙

JOE CANNON'S FAVORITE CARROT CAKE

Joe Cannon

Makes 1 (13x9-inch) cake

3 eggs
2 cups sugar
1 cup vegetable oil

1 teaspoon baking soda
3 cups flour
1 teaspoon cinnamon
1 teaspoon salt
2 cups grated carrots
1 (8 ounce) can crushed pineapple,
   with juice
2 teaspoons vanilla

FROSTING
8 ounces cream cheese
½ cup butter
1 teaspoon vanilla
1 pound powdered sugar

In a large bowl mix eggs, sugar and oil well. Combine baking soda, flour, cinnamon and salt, and add to egg mixture. Mix well. Stir in carrots, pineapple and vanilla. Pour into greased and floured 9x13-inch baking pan. Bake at 375° for 1 hour. Done when toothpick comes out clean. Frost.

FROSTING   Combine cream cheese, butter, vanilla, and sugar. Mix well.

SCRIPTURE CAKE

Esther Fairman

Serves 10-12

1 cup Psalms 55:21
   (butter)
2 cups Jeremiah 6:20
   (sugar)
2 cups Nahum 3:12
   (chopped figs)
6 Jeremiah 17:11
   (eggs, beaten)

½ cup Judges 4:19
   (milk)
4 cups First Kings 4:22
   (flour)
Dash of Leviticus 2:13
   (salt)
2 teaspoons Amos 4:5
   (baking powder)
2 teaspoons Second Chronicles 9:9
   (allspice)
2 tablespoons First Samuel 14:25
   (honey)
2 cups First Samuel 30:12
   (figs or raisins)
1 cup Numbers 17:8
   (chopped almonds)

Cream butter and sugar. Add chopped figs. Combine eggs and milk. Sift together flour, salt, baking powder and allspice. Add flour mixture to creamed mixture alternately with egg mixture. Add honey and follow Solomon's prescription for making a good boy (Proverbs 23:14). Beat well. Stir in raisins and almonds. Pour into greased 9x13-inch pan and bake at 375° for 45 minutes.

❧✿✦❧

WISCONSIN CRANBERRY CAKE WITH HOT BUTTER SAUCE

Melvin Laird
Former Secretary of Defense

Serves 6-8

1½ tablespoons Wisconsin butter, melted
½ cup sugar
1 Wisconsin egg, beaten
1 cup flour, sifted
1½ teaspoons baking powder
½ teaspoon salt
½ cup Wisconsin milk
1 large cup fresh Wisconsin cranberries

SAUCE
½ cup Wisconsin butter
1 cup sugar
½ cup Wisconsin cream
1 teaspoon vanilla

In a large bowl cream together butter and sugar. Add egg. Combine flour, baking powder and salt. Add alternately to the creamed mixture with milk. Stir in cranberries. Pour into greased and floured 9-inch square pan. Bake at 350° for 30 minutes.

SAUCE In medium saucepan combine butter, sugar and cream. Cook at a slow boil for 10 minutes stirring frequently. Add vanilla. Sauce should be served hot. Suggestion: Use double boiler to keep sauce hot.

APPLE DOLLY CAKE

Jane Chesley

Serves 8

½ cup butter
1 cup sugar

1 egg, well beaten
1½ cups flour, sifted
1 teaspoon baking soda
¼ teaspoon salt
1 teaspoon cinnamon
¼ teaspoon nutmeg
½ teaspoon cloves
½ cup strong, cold coffee
1 cup chopped apples
1 cup chopped walnuts
1 cup raisins

In a large bowl cream together butter and sugar. Add egg and blend well. Sift together flour, baking soda, salt, cinnamon, nutmeg and cloves. Add dry ingredients to creamed mixture alternately with coffee. Stir in apples, nuts and raisins. Pour into greased and floured 11x7-inch pan. Bake at 350° for 35 minutes. Frost with boiled icing or powdered sugar

❦

PUMPKIN CAKE

Janet Leigh Brandt

Serves 10

2 cups sugar
1¼ cups oil
4 eggs
2¼ cups buttermilk biscuit mix

2 teaspoons cinnamon
½ teaspoon nutmeg
1 (16 ounce) can pumpkin
1 tablespoon triple sec
¾ cup golden raisins
1 cup chopped walnuts

CREAM CHEESE FROSTING
½ cup unsalted butter, softened
8 ounces cream cheese, softened
1 teaspoon vanilla
½ teaspoon lemon extract
1 pound powdered sugar, sifted

Cream sugar and 1 cup oil until smooth. Add eggs one at a time, beating after each addition. Mix 2 cups biscuit mix with cinnamon and nutmeg. Add to creamed mixture and mix until smooth. Add pumpkin and triple sec and mix thoroughly. Mix raisins and nuts with remaining ¼ cup each of oil and biscuit mix. Gently stir into cake batter.

Pour mixture into 2 greased and floured 9-inch round layer cake pans. Bake at 325° for 30-35 minutes or until cake is done. Cool a few minutes before turning out onto racks to cool completely.

CREAM CHEESE FROSTING   Cream butter and cheese until smooth. Beat in vanilla, lemon extract, and slowly add sugar, beating well.

This recipe is a Thanksgiving or Christmas version of carrot cake. The triple sec brings out the flavor of pumpkin.

OLD-FASHIONED DATE CAKE

Lorie Luber

Serves 8

1 cup sugar
4 tablespoons butter
1 egg, beaten
1 cup flour

¼ teaspoon salt
1 teaspoon baking soda
½ teaspoon nutmeg
½ teaspoon cinnamon
1 cup diced dates
2 cups peeled and chopped apples
½ cup chopped nuts
¾ cup buttermilk

CREAM CHEESE FROSTING
4 tablespoons butter, softened
4 ounces cream cheese, softened
½ teaspoon vanilla
½ pound powdered sugar

Cream together butter and sugar until light and fluffy. Add beaten egg and mix well. In a separate bowl, combine flour, salt, baking soda, nutmeg and cinnamon.

Place dates in a sieve and run hot water over them for a few minutes to absorb moisture. Drain well. Add dates, apples and nuts to dry ingredients. Add date mixture to creamed mixture alternately with buttermilk.

Pour into greased and floured 9x9-inch cake pan. Bake at 350° for 45-50 minutes. When cool, frost with CREAM CHEESE FROSTING.

CREAM CHEESE FROSTING   Cream together butter and cream cheese. Add vanilla and powdered sugar. Beat well.

A fun holiday cake and a good replacement for pumpkin pie.

NEW JERSEY STYLE CHEESECAKE

John Meadows

Serves 10-12

32 ounces cream cheese, whipped
16 ounces sour cream
½ cup unsalted butter, softened
1¼ cups sugar
1 teaspoon lemon juice
1¼ teaspoons vanilla
2 tablespoons cornstarch
5 eggs

In a large bowl, combine cream cheese, sour cream and butter. Mix on high speed until thoroughly blended. Continue beating, and add sugar, lemon juice, vanilla and cornstarch. Add one egg at a time, mixing thoroughly after each addition.

Pour into a well greased 9-inch springform pan. Place pan in a larger roasting pan filled with water to half springform pan depth. Bake at 375° for exactly 1 hour. Top of cake should be golden brown.

Turn off oven, open door and allow cake to cool in oven for 1 hour. Remove from water bath and allow cake to cool on counter 2 hours. Refrigerate at least 6 hours before serving.

PRUNE CAKE
Betty Osborne

Makes 1 (9x13-inch) cake

1 cup butter
1½ cups sugar
3 eggs
1 teaspoon cinnamon
1 teaspoon nutmeg
1 teaspoon allspice

1 teaspoon baking soda
1½ cups flour
1 cup buttermilk
1 teaspoon vanilla
1 cup nuts
2 cups chopped prunes

BUTTERMILK ICING
1 cup sugar
½ cup buttermilk
½ teaspoon baking soda
1 tablespoon light corn syrup
¼ cup butter
1 teaspoon vanilla

In a large bowl, beat together butter and sugar. Add eggs one at a time, beating well after each addition. In a separate bowl combine cinnamon, nutmeg, allspice, baking soda and flour. Add dry ingredients to creamed mixture alternately with buttermilk, stirring until blended after each addition. Add vanilla, nuts and prunes. Pour into greased 9x13-inch pan and bake at 300° for 45 minutes. Cover with BUTTERMILK ICING while hot.

BUTTERMILK ICING Combine sugar, buttermilk, soda, corn syrup, butter and vanilla in a medium saucepan. Heat stirring constantly until icing reaches soft ball stage. Pour over hot cake without beating.

❦

CHOCOLATE MOUSSE PIE
Peter Weiss
Peter's Restaurant

Serves 12

CRUST
2½ cups graham cracker crumbs
4 ounces bitter chocolate, grated
¼ cup sugar
½ cup melted butter

FILLING
8 ounces semi-sweet chocolate
2 whole eggs
2 egg yolks
2 cups heavy cream
½ cup powdered sugar
4 egg whites, beaten stiff

CRUST Combine ingredients and press into 10-inch springform pan. Refrigerate.

FILLING Melt chocolate in double boiler. Beat in eggs and yolks. Whip cream, incorporating sugar. Fold into chocolate mixture, then fold in beaten egg whites. Turn into crust. Chill 6 hours. Garnish with whipped cream and strawberries.

CHOCOLATE CHEESECAKE

Billie Smardon

Serves 12

CRUST
1 (6 ounce) box Zwieback toast
2 tablespoons sugar
1½ teaspoons cinnamon
½ cup butter, melted

FILLING
3 (8 ounce) packages cream cheese
1 cup sugar
3 eggs
½ teaspoon vanilla
2 ounces German sweet chocolate,
 finely grated

TOPPING
2 cups sour cream
2 tablespoons sugar
½ teaspoon vanilla
1 ounce German chocolate, finely grated

CRUST   Crush toast to fine crumbs. Add sugar, cinnamon and melted butter. Mix well and press into bottom and sides of a 9-inch springform mold.

FILLING   Beat cream cheese until light, add sugar gradually and continue to beat. Add eggs, one at a time, beating after each addition. Add vanilla and stir in grated chocolate. Spoon into crust. Bake at 375° for 20 minutes. It should not be firm in the center. Cool completely. Reduce oven temperature to 350°.

TOPPING   Beat together sour cream, sugar and vanilla. Spoon over cooled cheesecake and bake at 350° for 10 minutes. Cool and refrigerate overnight. Before serving, sprinkle 1 ounce grated chocolate over the top of the cake. Slice and serve.

Needs to be refrigerated overnight.

❦

CREAM CHEESE PIE

Becky Dittmer

Serves 8

8 ounces cream cheese, softened
½ cup sugar

1 tablespoon lemon juice
½ teaspoon vanilla
Dash of salt
2 eggs
1 graham cracker crust
1 cup sour cream
½ teaspoon vanilla
2 tablespoons sugar
Freezer jam

Beat cream cheese until fluffy. Gradually add ½ cup sugar, lemon juice, vanilla and salt. Add eggs one at a time beating well after each addition. Pour into crust. Bake at 325° for 35-40 minutes.

Combine sour cream, ½ teaspoon vanilla and 2 tablespoons sugar. Spoon over pie. Bake 10 minutes more. Cool then chill several hours. Top with favorite freezer jam and serve.

PATRIOTIC PIE
Kathleen Harriman Mortimer

Serves 6-8

1½ cups graham cracker crumbs
½ cup powdered sugar
⅛ teaspoon cinnamon
4 tablespoons melted butter
1 (8 ounce) jar currant jelly, softened
1 box fresh raspberries
1 box fresh blueberries
Powdered sugar or vanilla ice cream

Combine graham cracker crumbs, powdered sugar, cinnamon and butter. Mix well and press into bottom and sides of a 9-inch pie pan. Chill 1 hour. Spread currant jelly on inside of pie crust. Arrange blueberries and raspberries in a pattern on top of jelly.

Just before serving, dust with powdered sugar or dollops of ice cream, but be sure color of berries shows through.

Substitute all blueberries or all raspberries if desired.

DARK AND WHITE CHOCOLATE MOUSSE PIE
Barbara Young

Serves 6-8

6 ounces chocolate wafers
½ cup pecans
4 tablespoons well chilled butter
10 ounces semi-sweet chocolate
4 eggs, separated, at room temperature
¼ cup coffee liqueur
½ cup whipping cream
1 ounce white chocolate, grated

Generously butter a 10-inch pie pan. In bowl of food processor using steel blade, mix wafers, pecans and butter until texture of coarse meal. Press into bottom and sides of pie pan.

Melt semi-sweet chocolate in top of double boiler; set over gently simmering water. Blend in beaten egg yolks and liqueur. Transfer to large bowl.

In another large bowl, beat egg whites until stiff but not dry. Fold into chocolate mixture in three batches. In a medium size bowl beat cream until stiff. Blend in white chocolate.

Fill shell with half of chocolate mixture. Top with whipped cream mixture. Spoon remaining chocolate mixture, spreading evenly. Freeze at least 30 minutes before serving.

IMPOSSIBLE COCONUT PIE

Lisa Kettleband

Serves 8

4 eggs
4 tablespoons margarine
⅔ cup sugar
½ cup flour
¼ teaspoon salt
½ teaspoon baking powder
2 cups milk
1 cup shredded coconut
1 teaspoon vanilla
½ teaspoon coconut flavor

Combine all ingredients in container of blender. Mix well. Pour into greased and floured 10-inch pie plate. Bake at 350° for 45-60 minutes.

FRUIT COBBLER

Ruth Purdy

Serves 6

1 cup sugar
1 cup flour
2 teaspoons baking powder
⅛ teaspoon salt
1 egg
Milk
Peaches, or other fruit
Brown sugar

Mix together sugar, flour, baking powder, salt and egg with enough milk to make batter pour. Peel and slice peaches. Grease pan and put fruit in. Sprinkle with brown sugar. Pour batter over top of fruit.. Bake at 375° for 30 minutes.

PLUM KUCHEN

Mary Ann Ryan

Serves 8

½ cup butter
½ cup sugar
3 eggs
½ teaspoon vanilla
1 cup unsifted flour
14-16 Italian plums, quartered
2-3 tablespoons sugar

Butter and flour an 11-inch round pie plate. Cream together butter and sugar. Beat in eggs, one at a time. Stir in vanilla and flour. Pour mixture into prepared pie plate. Arrange plums closely together in a circle on top of mixture. Sprinkle fruit with 2-3 tablespoons sugar. Bake at 375° for 40 minutes.

Serve warm with vanilla ice cream.

BAVAROIS A L'ORANGE

Mr. and Mrs. Walter Annenberg
Former Ambassador
Court of St. James

Serves 8-10

4 cups milk
12 egg yolks
1 cup sugar
4 envelopes unflavored gelatin
1½ cups whipping cream
Juice and rind of 2 oranges

½ cup Grand Marnier
3 teaspoons vanilla

DECORATION
2 cups sugar
½ cup water
8 orange wedges
8 strawberries
1 cup whipping cream, whipped
Roasted almonds

SAUCE
1 jar apricot preserves
Juice of 3 oranges
Juice of 1 lemon
Rind of 1 orange
Grand Marnier

Heat milk to almost boiling. In another saucepan beat the 12 egg yolks with sugar. When well whipped add the gelatin, then gradually add the milk, mixing thoroughly. Return to stove. Heat carefully stirring constantly until the mixture coats the spoon. Strain mixture into a bowl and let cool, stirring from time to time. Meanwhile, beat whipping cream until firm and chill.

When the first mixture is cooled and becomes a little firm, add orange juice and rind, Grand Marnier, vanilla and whipped cream. Mix together and put into wet mold in refrigerator until set. This dish should be set in the refrigerator at least 2-3 hours before serving.

DECORATION   Place sugar and water in saucepan and heat until carmelized. Grease marble slab with small amount of oil. Dip oranges and strawberries in caramel and place on oiled marble. Turn the mold out into a serving dish and decorate with whipped cream using piping bag.

Place carmelized fruit around the mold and sprinkle with almonds. Serve with sauce.

SAUCE   Put first three ingredients together in a saucepan and simmer 5-10 minutes; strain and let cool. When cold, add rind of 1 orange and a little Grand Marnier.

ALMOND CHOCO SEMIFREDDO

Linda Fairfield

Serves 8-10

4 ounces chocolate, chopped
1 cup hand-crushed Amaretto cookies
1 cup chopped, toasted almonds
4 eggs, separated
⅛ teaspoon salt
1 cup sugar
2 cups whipping cream, whipped stiff
3 tablespoons Amaretto
2 tablespoons vanilla

Line the bottom of a 9-inch springform pan with foil. Combine chocolate, cookies and almonds. Set aside.

In a medium bowl, beat egg whites and salt to soft peaks. In a separate bowl beat egg yolks. Gradually add sugar and continue beating until thick and lemon colored. Fold egg whites into egg yolks. Add Amaretto and vanilla to whipped cream and fold gently into egg mixture.

Sprinkle ⅓ of cookie mixture on bottom of springform pan. Top with half of cream mixture. Sprinkle with ⅓ cookie mixture. Top with remaining half cream mixture. Sprinkle with remaining cookie mixture. Cover and freeze for 12 hours.

FROZEN GRAND MARNIER MOUSSE

Ruth Jones

Serves 6

2 egg whites
⅛ teaspoon salt
¼ cup sugar
1 cup whipping cream
2 tablespoons sugar
¼ cup Grand Marnier or Cherry Heering

Beat egg whites with salt until soft peaks form. Gradually add ¼ cup sugar and beat until stiff and shiny.

In a separate bowl whip cream until stiff. Add 2 tablespoons sugar, then gently blend in Grand Marnier.

Gently fold whipped cream mixture into beaten egg whites. Turn into 1 quart mold and freeze until firm.

DELIGHTFUL STRAWBERRY SOUFFLÉ

Valerie Dumke

Serves 10-12

CRUST
2 cups flour
1 cup chopped pecans
1 cup butter, melted
½ cup brown sugar

FILLING
1 (10 ounce) package sweetened frozen
    strawberries, thawed
1 cup sugar
2 teaspoons fresh lemon juice
2 egg whites, room temperature
1 cup whipping cream, whipped stiff

In a 9x13-inch baking pan, combine flour, pecans, butter and brown sugar. Stir well. Bake at 350° for 30 minutes, stirring occasionally. Cool.

In a large mixing bowl, combine strawberries, sugar, lemon juice and egg whites. Beat at high speed of an electric mixer for 10-12 minutes or until very stiff peaks form. Fold in whipped cream.

Press about one-half to two-thirds of crumb mixture into a 9½-inch springform pan. Spoon in strawberry mixture. Sprinkle remaining crumbs on top and freeze until firm. Garnish with fresh strawberries if desired.

SORBET RHUBARBE

Mrs. W. Averell Harriman

Makes 1 quart plus

4 cups chopped rhubarb
½ cup water
1 scant cup superfine sugar
½ cup light corn syrup
½ cup orange juice
3 tablespoons fresh lemon juice

Place rhubarb and water in a saucepan and cook, covered, until tender, about 5 minutes. Do not drain. Transfer mixture to food processor or blender. Add sugar, corn syrup, orange juice and lemon juice and purée until smooth. Freeze mixture in an ice cream freezer according to machine instructions, or freeze in a flat pan until nearly set. Beat until smooth and re-freeze.

Bright pink rhubarb will have the best color and flavor, but if necessary you can add a little red food coloring to the purée.

BAKED FUDGE DESSERT

Jane Elliot

Serves 8-10

4 eggs, well beaten
2 cups sugar
½ cup flour
½ cup cocoa
1 cup butter, melted
2 teaspoons vanilla
1 cup chopped pecans
Whipped cream or ice cream

In a large bowl beat eggs well. Mix together the sugar, flour and cocoa. Add to the beaten eggs and blend thoroughly. Add butter, vanilla and nuts. Pour into greased and floured 9x9-inch pan. Place in a pan of hot water. Bake at 300° for 45 minutes or until knife inserted in center comes out clean. It will have the consistency of custard. When cool, cut into squares and serve with whipped cream or ice cream.

May be made a day ahead.

LEMON DESSERT

Lynette Nance

Serves 12

1 cup flour
½ cup butter, softened
½ cup chopped walnuts

1 cup whipping cream, whipped
  (or La Creme)
1 cup powdered sugar
1 (8 ounce) package cream cheese
Dash of salt
2 (3½ ounce) packages instant
  lemon pudding
3 cups cold milk
Whipped cream
Chopped walnuts

Mix together flour, butter and walnuts. Press into the bottom of a 9x13-inch pan. Bake at 350° for 15 minutes. Cool thoroughly.

Whip together whipped cream, powdered sugar, cream cheese and salt. Spread over cooled crumb mixture. Chill 15-30 minutes.

Mix together lemon pudding mix and milk. Pour over cream cheese mixture. Chill. Garnish with additional whipped cream and chopped walnuts. Keep refrigerated.

ORANGE SOUFFLÉ

Joan Danforth

Serves 4-6

4 egg whites
4 tablespoons sugar
3 tablespoons orange marmalade
Grated rind of 1 orange
¼ teaspoon orange extract

SAUCE
4 egg yolks
1 cup powdered sugar
1 cup heavy cream
1 tablespoon rum or brandy

Beat egg whites until stiff but not dry. Beat in sugar and fold in marmalade, orange rind, and orange extract. Cook 1 hour in a buttered double boiler. Turn out on serving dish and serve with SAUCE.

SAUCE Beat egg yolks well and add powdered sugar. Whip 1 cup heavy cream and add rum or brandy. Mix into egg yolk.

ORANGE PUDDING

Jane Ramlow

Serves 4-6

2 medium oranges, peeled and sectioned
⅓ cup sugar

2 tablespoons cornstarch
⅛ teaspoon salt
2 cups milk, scalded
2 egg yolks, beaten
2 egg whites, stiffly beaten
1 teaspoon vanilla
Whipped cream
½-1 teaspoon orange liqueur

Put oranges in a large bowl and sprinkle with small amount of sugar. Set aside. Mix sugar, cornstarch and salt. Add scalded milk. Cook mixture in top of double boiler stirring constantly for 15 minutes. Add beaten egg yolks. Cook and stir until smooth, about 2 minutes. Remove from heat and fold in egg whites. Add vanilla.

While mixture is still warm, pour over oranges and mix. Refrigerate and serve cold topped with whipped cream flavored with orange liqueur.

OLD-FASHIONED RICE PUDDING

Wordell Rainey
Mayor of Hailey

Serves 6-8

6 cups milk
¾ cup sugar
¼ teaspoon salt
1 tablespoon butter or margarine
¾ cup raisins
3-4 eggs
2 cups cooked rice
1 teaspoon vanilla
  or ½ teaspoon coconut flavoring
  and ¼ teaspoon vanilla
Cinnamon

In a large saucepan, combine milk, sugar, salt, butter and raisins. Heat just to boiling point. In a large bowl beat eggs well. While beating constantly, slowly add milk mixture. Add rice and vanilla.

Pour into 2 quart casserole and sprinkle with cinnamon. Put casserole in pan of hot water and bake at 325° for 60-75 minutes or until center is firm.

APPLE PUDDING

Lois Glenn

Serves 6-8

1 cup flour
1 teaspoon baking soda
1 teaspoon cinnamon
¼ cup shortening
1 cup sugar

¼ teaspoon salt
1 teaspoon vanilla
1 egg
½ cup chopped nuts
3 apples, grated

SAUCE
½ cup sugar
½ cup brown sugar
¼ cup butter
½ cup evaporated milk or light cream
1 teaspoon vanilla

Sift together flour, soda and cinnamon. In a separate bowl cream shortening with sugar, salt, vanilla and egg. Add flour mixture stirring just until blended. Stir in nuts and apples. Pour into greased 9x5-inch bread pan, and bake at 350° for 45 minutes. Cool.

SAUCE Combine sugars, butter, milk and vanilla. Bring mixture barely to a boil. Immediately remove from heat. Pour warm sauce over pudding at serving time.

THE BEST CHOCOLATE CHIP COOKIES

Missy Butterfield

Makes approximately 8 dozen

1⅓ cups sugar
1 cup brown sugar
4 eggs
1 tablespoon vanilla
1 tablespoon lemon juice
2 teaspoons baking soda
1½ teaspoons salt
1 teaspoon ground cinnamon
½ cup rolled oats
3 cups flour
2 (12 ounce) packages semi-sweet
   chocolate chips
2 cups chopped walnuts

1 cup shortening (Crisco)
½ cup butter

In a large mixing bowl, combine shortening, butter and sugars. Beat on high speed until thoroughly combined, about 5 minutes. Beat in eggs one at a time, beating well after each addition. Add vanilla and lemon juice.

In a separate bowl, stir together baking soda, salt, cinnamon, oats and flour. Beat dry ingredients into creamed mixture until well blended. Stir in chocolate chips and nuts.

Drop by small tablespoonsful onto lightly greased baking sheet about 3 inches apart. Bake at 350° for 16-18 minutes or until golden brown. Cool on wire rack.

AUNT SALLY'S COCOA DROPS

Mary Ann Flaherty

1 cup sugar
1 egg
¾ cup buttermilk or sour milk
1 teaspoon vanilla
1¾ cups flour, sifted
½ teaspoon baking soda
½ teaspoon salt
½ cup cocoa
1 cup chopped nuts

¼ cup soft shortening
¼ cup butter

In a large bowl combine shortening, butter, sugar and egg. Beat well. Stir in buttermilk and vanilla. Sift together flour, baking soda, salt and cocoa. Stir into creamed mixture. Stir in nuts. Chill dough 1 hour.

Drop by tablespoonsful 2 inches apart onto a lightly greased cookie sheet. Bake at 400° for 8-10 minutes. Cool. Frost with chocolate icing.

HEALTHY HONEY BRAN COOKIES

Ellen Fisher

Makes 3 dozen

1 cup whole wheat pastry flour
¼ teaspoon baking powder
½ teaspoon baking soda
¼ teaspoon salt
½ teaspoon cinnamon
¼ teaspoon cloves (optional)
½ cup butter
½ cup honey
1 teaspoon vanilla
1 egg
¾ cup unprocessed bran
½ cup chopped nuts or sunflower seeds
½ cup raisins

Sift together flour, baking powder, baking soda, salt, cinnamon and cloves. Cream butter and gradually add honey. Add vanilla and egg to creamed mixture and beat well. Stir flour mixture and bran into batter gradually. Add nuts and raisins. Drop from teaspoons onto ungreased cookie sheet. Bake at 350° for 10-12 minutes.

MONTE CARLOS

Clara Spiegel

Makes 30 biscuits

10 tablespoons butter, cubed
½ cup sugar
1 egg
2 teaspoons honey
½ teaspoon vanilla
2¼ cups self-rising flour
¼ cup coconut

FILLING
4 tablespoons butter, cubed
½ teaspoon vanilla
1¼ cups powdered sugar
2-3 tablespoons apricot jam

Cream butter with sugar in a blender or food processor. Add egg, honey and vanilla, and process a few seconds. Add flour and coconut and process to combine. Take teaspoonsful of the mixture, roll into balls, place on greased cookie sheet, and flatten slightly with a fork. Bake at 350° for 10 minutes or until pale golden brown.

FILLING Process butter, vanilla, powdered sugar and apricot or other jam. When biscuits are done, spread the flat underside of half of them with the jam filling. Sandwich them together with the flat side of another unspread biscuit.

Serve them with an ice sherbet or other cool, sweet dessert.

FROSTED SOUR CREAM COOKIES

Judy Jones

Makes 10 dozen

1 cup butter
2 cups sugar
2 eggs
2 teaspoons vanilla
5⅓ cups flour
2 teaspoons baking powder
1 teaspoon baking soda
1 teaspoon salt
½ teaspoon nutmeg
1 cup sour cream

In a large bowl cream butter, sugar, eggs and vanilla. In a separate bowl, sift together flour, baking powder, soda, salt and nutmeg. Add to the creamed mixture alternately with sour cream. Chill dough 1 hour. Roll dough out to ¼-inch thickness. Cut into desired shapes. Bake at 425° for 8-10 minutes or until lightly browned. Frost with CREAM CHEESE FROSTING (see index).

GOLDEN ALMOND CRISP

Sue Peterson

Makes 7½ dozen

1 cup butter
1 cup sugar
1 egg
1 tablespoon lemon rind
2 tablespoons rum
3 cups sifted flour
½ teaspoon baking powder
¼ cup sugar
¼ teaspoon cinnamon
½ cup finely chopped almonds
1 egg white, slightly beaten

Cream together butter and sugar. Beat in egg, lemon rind and rum, mixing well. Sift together flour and baking powder and add to creamed mixture. Mix well. Roll into ball and chill, wrapped in waxed paper, for 1 hour.

Mix together ¼ cup sugar, cinnamon and almonds. Roll chilled dough out into ⅛-inch thickness. Cut into 2-inch rounds. Brush with egg white and sprinkle with cinnamon-almond mixture. Bake at 325° for 12 minutes. Cool on wire racks.

BLONDE BROWNIES
Maxine N. Smith

Makes 24 bars

⅓ cup butter, melted
1 cup brown sugar
1 egg, slightly beaten
1 teaspoon vanilla
1 cup flour
½ teaspoon baking powder
⅛ teaspoon baking soda
½ teaspoon salt
½ cup chopped nuts
1 (6 ounce) package semi-sweet
   chocolate chips

In a mixing bowl blend together melted butter and sugar. Beat in egg and vanilla. Combine flour, baking powder, baking soda and salt. Gradually add to butter mixture until well blended. Stir in nuts. Spread mixture in greased 9x9-inch pan. Sprinkle chocolate chips over top. Bake at 350° for 20-25 minutes. Cool in pan. Cut into bars.

❧❀◖◗❀❧

SUN VALLEY'S FAMOUS BUTTERSCOTCH BROWNIES
Sun Valley Company

Makes 36 (2-inch) squares

3 cups brown sugar
1 cup margarine
¼ cup water
1½ cups brown sugar
5 eggs
Dash of vanilla
3¾ cups cake flour
2 teaspoons baking powder
1½ cups chopped walnuts
Butterscotch chips

In a double boiler heat 3 cups brown sugar, margarine, and water into a butterscotch mixture.

In a large bowl beat remaining brown sugar, eggs and vanilla. Add butterscotch mixture a little at a time, beat on low speed, scraping down in between each addition. Add flour, baking powder and nuts. Mix all ingredients until well incorporated. Spread into a well greased 12x12-inch pan. Sprinkle with butterscotch chips. Bake at 375° for 25 minutes.

WALNUT SQUARES

Joan Gaughran

Makes 24 squares

2½ cups flour
1 cup butter
4 eggs slightly beaten
3 cups brown sugar

1 cup coconut
2 cups chopped walnuts
4 tablespoons flour
½ teaspoon baking powder
1 teaspoon salt
2 teaspoons vanilla

ICING
½ cup butter
2 cups powdered sugar
4 tablespoons orange juice
1 teaspoon lemon juice
½ cup chopped walnuts

Mix flour and butter into a paste. Spread on a 10x16-inch cookie sheet, and bake at 350° for 20-25 minutes or until light brown. Meanwhile mix eggs, brown sugar, coconut, walnuts, flour, baking powder, salt and vanilla. Spread over crust and bake at 350° for 20 minutes. Cool.

ICING   Mix together butter, sugar, orange juice and lemon juice. Frost crust and sprinkle with nuts. Cut into squares.

BREAKFAST BARS

Elaine McClure

Makes 48 bars

½ cup light corn syrup
½ cup chunky peanut butter
½ cup butter or margarine, melted
⅓ cup brown sugar
2 cups quick oats
2 cups granola
1 cup raisins
1 (6 ounce) package semi-sweet
   chocolate chips

Combine corn syrup, peanut butter, butter, sugar, oats, granola and raisins. Press mixture into greased 9x13-inch pan. Bake at 350° for 20 minutes. Top with chocolate chips. Return cookies to oven until chips melt. Spread over cookies. Let stand a few minutes, cut and remove from pan.

Great kids' cookies.

CHINESE CHEWS

Helen Miller

Makes 40 Chews

CRUST
2 cups plus 2 tablespoons flour
1 cup unsalted butter
1 cup brown sugar

TOPPING
1½ cups brown sugar
¼ teaspoon salt
2 eggs
1 teaspoon vanilla
½ teaspoon baking soda
1 cup coarsely chopped pecans

CRUST   Combine flour, butter and brown sugar. Mix well. Press into 9x13-inch baking pan. Bake at 300° for 10 minutes.

TOPPING   Combine brown sugar, salt, eggs, vanilla, baking soda and pecans. Mix well. Spread over hot crust. Return to oven and bake 30-35 minutes or until light brown. Cool and cut into small squares.

TRIPLE TREAT CHEWS

Clarice Blechmann

Makes 8 dozen (1-inch) squares

CRUST
1½ cups flour
½ cup brown sugar
1 tablespoon grated orange rind

¼ teaspoon salt
½ cup butter
1 (6 ounce) package semi-sweet
   chocolate chips

TOPPING
2 eggs
¼ cup flour
1 cup brown sugar
¼ teaspoon salt
½ teaspoon baking powder
1 teaspoon vanilla
1½ cups chopped walnuts

CRUST   In a large bowl combine flour, brown sugar, orange rind and salt. Cut in butter with a pastry blender until mixture is crumbly. Press evenly over bottom of an ungreased 9x13-inch baking pan. Bake at 375° for 10 minutes or until firm. Sprinkle chocolate pieces over crust in pan. Let stand 2 minutes. Spread chocolate evenly over pastry.

TOPPING   In a medium bowl beat eggs until thick. Stir in flour, sugar, salt, baking powder, vanilla and walnuts. Spread over chocolate layer. Bake at 375° for 20 minutes or until top is golden. Cool completely in pan.

POLLY'S APPLE LEMON BARS

Mrs. Gene Biedebach

1 cup plus 2 tablespoons shortening
2¾ cups unbleached flour
1 teaspoon salt
Milk

1 egg yolk, slightly beaten
1 cup crushed 40% bran flakes
Grated rind of 1-2 lemons
7-8 cups thinly sliced apples
⅔ cup sugar
½ teaspoon cinnamon
¼ teaspoon allspice
1-2 tablespoons lemon juice
1 egg white
1 cup powdered sugar
½ teaspoon vanilla
Juice of 2 lemons
3 tablespoons finely chopped nuts

Cut shortening into flour and salt until particles are size of small peas. Add enough milk to egg yolk to measure ⅔ cup. Stir into flour mixture. Divide pastry into 2 balls. Flatten and roll on lightly floured board into 2 (15x10-inch) rectangles. Fold into thirds, and put into 15x10-inch jelly roll pan. Unfold to cover bottom of pan. Sprinkle with crushed cereal and grated lemon rind. Do not skimp on grated lemon rind.

Mix apples with sugar, cinnamon and allspice. Sprinkle with 1-2 tablespoons lemon juice. Spread over cereal. Cover with second pastry rectangle. Beat egg white until soft peaks form. Brush over pastry. Bake at 350° for 55-60 minutes or until crust is golden brown.

Combine powdered sugar, vanilla and juice of 2 lemons. Mix until smooth and creamy. Add more lemon juice if needed. Spread over warm crust and sprinkle with nuts. Cut into bars.

GIFTS

CRISPY SUGAR WALNUTS

Mary Ellen Ivy

Makes 3 cups

2½ cups walnut halves
1 cup sugar
½ cup water
1 teaspoon cinnamon
½ teaspoon salt
1½ teaspoons vanilla

Heat walnuts in a 350° oven for 5 minutes, stirring once. Cook remaining ingredients, except vanilla, over medium heat until mixture reaches soft ball stage (236°) on candy thermometer. Remove from heat. Beat by hand 1 minute or until mixture just begins to get creamy. Add vanilla and walnuts. Stir to coat. Turn out onto a buttered platter or wax paper sheet and separate. Allow to cool.

A nice Christmas gift in pretty tins or boxes.

AMAZING PRALINES

JoAnn Levy

Makes 24 cookies

1 cup butter
1 cup brown sugar
1 cup chopped pecans
12 graham cracker squares

Lightly grease the bottom of a 13x9-inch pan. Line the bottom with whole graham crackers. Bring butter and brown sugar to a slow boil over medium high heat until mixture is clear and bubbly. Add chopped pecans to mixture. Spread evenly over graham crackers making sure all of crackers are evenly covered. Place in oven and bake at 400° for 5 minutes or until bubbly. Remove from oven and let cool for 5 minutes. While still warm, cut into bite-size pieces.

ALMOND ROCCA

Bonnie Williams

2 cups walnuts, finely chopped
1 pound chocolate bars, chopped
2 cups butter
2¼ cups sugar
1½-2 cups whole almonds

Lightly butter 9x13-inch jelly roll pan. Sprinkle half of walnuts on bottom of pan. Sprinkle half of chocolate on walnuts. In a medium size heavy weight saucepan, combine butter and sugar. Stirring constantly, heat over medium-high heat until mixture reaches 300° on a candy thermometer. At this point drain off clarified butter which has risen to the top. Add almonds and pour mixture over chocolate. Sprinkle on remaining chocolate and walnuts. Let cool and break into pieces.

LILLIAN'S FUDGE

Loretta Williams

Makes 5 pounds

4½ cups sugar
13 ounces evaporated milk
18 ounces semisweet chocolate chips
1 ounce marshmallow cream
1 cup butter or margarine
2 teaspoons vanilla
2 cups chopped nuts

Boil sugar and milk together and cook 10 minutes over lower heat, stirring constantly. Remove from heat, and add chocolate chips, marshmallow cream, butter, vanilla and nuts. Stir until thick.

Pour mixture into 9x13-inch buttered baking pan. Cool to room temperature. Refrigerate overnight and cut into squares.

DA LA'S MUSTARD À LA WOODSIDE

Carol Jones

1 cup malt vinegar
4 ounces dry mustard
1 cup sugar
6 eggs

Mix vinegar and dry mustard together, and let stand in the top of a double boiler for 2 hours. Beat together sugar and eggs. Cook vinegar and mustard in double boiler, starting with cold water in the bottom of the boiler. Add eggs and sugar, cook until thickened, stirring constantly, about 10 minutes. If lumpy, beat with a rotary beater.

PERSIMMON COOKIES

Carla Carlisle

Makes 2½ dozen

½ cup butter
1 cup sugar

1 egg
1 cup persimmon pulp,
   with core and skin
1 teaspoon baking soda
2 cups flour
1 teaspoon cinnamon
½ teaspoon cloves
½ teaspoon nutmeg
½ teaspoon salt
1 cup raisins
1 cup chopped walnuts

In a large bowl cream together butter and sugar. Beat in egg. Sprinkle persimmon pulp with baking soda and beat into creamed mixture.

Combine flour, cinnamon, cloves, nutmeg and salt and beat into persimmon mixture. Stir in raisins and nuts. Drop dough by tablespoonsful onto greased cookie sheets. Bake at 375° for 15 minutes.

Cookies are very good, spicy, and moist. They freeze well and make it through the mail without the usual crumbling.

SMALL PRETZEL COOKIES

Cheri Drougas

4 cups sifted flour
1 teaspoon cream of tartar
1½ cups butter
1 cup light cream
1 egg, beaten
½ cup sugar

In a large bowl combine flour with cream of tartar. With pastry blender or two knives, cut in butter until like cornmeal. Add cream, a little at a time; blend well. Refrigerate 1 hour.

With palms of hands, roll dough into several pencil-shaped rolls ¼-inch thick on a lightly floured board; then cut each roll into pieces 8½-inches long. Shape each piece into a pretzel, then dip in egg, then into sugar. Place, coated side up, on lightly greased cookie sheet. Bake at 400° for 20 minutes or until light golden brown.

GRANOLA

Penny Mazzola

Makes 3 quarts

3 cups rolled oats
2 cups rye or wheat flakes
1 cup sunflower seeds
1 cup slivered almonds

1 cup shredded or sliced coconut
2 cups raw wheat germ
½ teaspoon salt
1 cup non-fat dry milk powder
½ cup sesame seeds
½ teaspoon cinnamon
¼ teaspoon ground cloves
½ cup honey or syrup
1 cup corn or peanut oil
1 cup raisins

In a large bowl mix all ingredients except honey, oil and raisins. Divide into 2 batches. Place in 2 large pans with sides. Over each pan drizzle half the oil, then half the honey. Stir with a fork. Bake at 250° for 30 minutes, removing every 10 minutes to stir thoroughly. When cooked add raisins.

HOT FUDGE SAUCE

Vance Carter
Copper Basin Restaurant

4 cups whipping cream
4 ounces unsweetened chocolate
Powdered sugar
Brandy or Grand Marnier

Combine cream and chocolate in a heavy saucepan and melt slowly. Add powdered sugar to thicken Remove from heat and add brandy or Grand Marnier.

HOT BUTTERED RUM

Heidi Heath

BATTER
½ pound melted butter
½ pound brown sugar
1 pint melted vanilla ice cream
¼ teaspoon nutmeg
¼ teaspoon cinnamon

1 cup boiling water
2 teaspoons batter
1 shot rum or brandy
Freshly grated nutmeg

BATTER   Mix butter and sugar until blended well. Stir in ice cream, then mix in nutmeg and cinnamon. Place in desired jars and freeze. Keep batter stored in freezer.

Mix together water, batter, and rum or brandy. Sprinkle with nutmeg.

Great for the holidays or use just a little batter mixed in a hot cup of tea.

RECIPE INDEX

RECIPE INDEX

RECIPE INDEX

RECIPE INDEX

RECIPE INDEX

RECIPE INDEX

RECIPE INDEX

RECIPE INDEX

RECIPE INDEX

RECIPE INDEX

RECIPE INDEX

RECIPE INDEX

RECIPE INDEX

RECIPE INDEX

RECIPE INDEX

RECIPE INDEX

RECIPE INDEX

Don "Bemco" Bennett

The landscape paintings of Don Bennett are the end result of years of formal art training coupled with a lifelong, first-hand knowledge of his subject - the outdoor West. A native of Idaho, he has lived and pursued his art in the Sun Valley area for the past 30 years. Depending on the season, skis or mountaineering boots are as essential as the painting gear he frequently backpacks into the mountains. His sketchbooks bulge with notes and drawings made from Montana to British Columbia, from Wyoming to the rain forests and beaches of the Pacific.

He has exhibited widely across the U.S. and abroad; hundreds of private collectors and many museums and institutions own "Bemco" paintings. Don Bennett's artistic achievements have won him the recognition of a listing in Who's Who in American Art and a biographical resume in Who's Who in the West.

Cover Illustration

Steve Snyder

As a child, Steve's playground was the site of one of the first steam-powered sawmills in the California Redwood forests, complete with deteriorating wagons, ox barns, yokes, a blacksmith's shop and a bellows from Russia. This gave him an appreciation of the early American West.

While in the Army, Steve bought a $20.00 pawnshop camera, and at a darkroom on base started processing film and prints. After gaining his college degree, Steve moved to the Sun Valley mountains. Here, he discovered his photography was documenting the bygone era of early western settlement. Along with capturing this disappearing history, he also became aware of Nature's beauty.

"Today I'm still trying to capture as much of the beauty, history and heritage of the world as I can and share it with others through my art."

Photography

SUN VALLEY COOKBOOK
MORITZ COMMUNITY HOSPITAL AUXILIARY
P.O. BOX 555
SUN VALLEY, IDAHO 83353

Please send me_____copies of **SUN VALLEY COOKBOOK** at $9.95* plus $2.00 postage and handling per copy.

Enclosed is my check for_____, payable to **Moritz Community Hospital Auxiliary.**

NAME _____

STREET _____

CITY _____ STATE _____ ZIP _____

The proceeds from the sale of this book will be returned to the **Moritz Community Hospital** through the Moritz Community Hospital Auxiliary.

*Idaho residents must add 40 cents (4%) tax per book.

☐ Please enclose gift card.   ☐ Do not enclose gift card.

SUN VALLEY COOKBOOK
MORITZ COMMUNITY HOSPITAL AUXILIARY
P.O. BOX 555
SUN VALLEY, IDAHO 83353

Please send me_____copies of **SUN VALLEY COOKBOOK** at $9.95* plus $2.00 postage and handling per copy.

Enclosed is my check for_____, payable to **Moritz Community Hospital Auxiliary.**

NAME _____

STREET _____

CITY _____ STATE _____ ZIP _____

The proceeds from the sale of this book will be returned to the **Moritz Community Hospital** through the Moritz Community Hospital Auxiliary.

*Idaho residents must add 40 cents (4%) tax per book.

☐ Please enclose gift card.   ☐ Do not enclose gift card.

Sun Valley Cookbook
MORITZ COMMUNITY HOSPITAL AUXILIARY
P.O. BOX 555
SUN VALLEY, IDAHO 83353

Please send me_____copies of **SUN VALLEY COOKBOOK** at $9.95* plus $2.00 postage and handling per copy.

Enclosed is my check for_____, payable to **Moritz Community Hospital Auxiliary.**

NAME_____

STREET_____

CITY_____STATE_____ZIP_____

The proceeds from the sale of this book will be returned to the **Moritz Community Hospital** through the Moritz Community Hospital Auxiliary.

*Idaho residents must add 40 cents (4%) tax per book.

☐ Please enclose gift card.   ☐ Do not enclose gift card.

Sun Valley Cookbook
MORITZ COMMUNITY HOSPITAL AUXILIARY
P.O. BOX 555
SUN VALLEY, IDAHO 83353

Please send me_____copies of **SUN VALLEY COOKBOOK** at $9.95* plus $2.00 postage and handling per copy.

Enclosed is my check for_____, payable to **Moritz Community Hospital Auxiliary.**

NAME_____

STREET_____

CITY_____STATE_____ZIP_____

The proceeds from the sale of this book will be returned to the **Moritz Community Hospital** through the Moritz Community Hospital Auxiliary.

*Idaho residents must add 40 cents (4%) tax per book.

☐ Please enclose gift card.   ☐ Do not enclose gift card.